How to Say No at Work

100 Essential Message Templates to Navigate Difficult Conversations and Establish Boundaries with Your Boss, Employees, and Coworkers

EMMA TAYLOR

DISCLAIMER!

The contents of the book "**How to Say No at Work**," including, but not limited to, the text, graphics, images, and other material contained within, are the exclusive property of the author and are protected under international copyright laws.

Table of Contents

INTRODUCTION

We live in a world that currently celebrates the power of yes. It's a trend: multiple websites, self-help books, and even novel and movie plots all claim that saying yes allows you to get more out of life. This mindset encourages cautious people seeking excitement or change to say yes rather than play things safe. In that sense, saying yes is often a wonderful thing. There's nothing wrong with saying yes when it gets you closer to your goals, such as finally taking that boxing class you've always wanted but were too afraid to sign up for, maintaining family harmony, or strategically strengthening your position at work. Saying yes at work is supposed to convey that you are a team player who supports your group and adds value to the organization. A yes is totally acceptable if it advances you in some way or makes you happy.

But here is the issue: "Yes." "Sure." "No problem." The words are out of your mouth before you realize how serious the commitment is. You learn too late that you don't want or have the time to do what you've committed to. You don't want to babysit for a friend's or sibling's children or have time to walk a neighbor's annoying dog whenever she asks. You're wondering how you got sucked into an extra workplace assignment or planned a coworker's farewell party. "How does this happen to me so often?" you might question. If you aren't wondering, maybe you should.

No, the term you repeated without hesitation at age two appears problematic, if not impossible, in many of your current conversations. It's time to reorient yourself to the word no. It can provide balance to your life and improve your interactions. By keeping no in mind, you have a plan and the ability to carry it out. With no, your well-being is prioritized.

THE IMPORTANCE OF SAYING NO

In the workplace, it's common to feel overwhelmed by various requests and obligations. Picture this: your colleagues and supervisors are all contributing ideas and tasks to your workload, leaving you feeling stretched thin. You may say yes to every assignment or suggestion, even when it doesn't align with your priorities or boundaries.

This scenario often leads to increased stress and dissatisfaction. Eventually, you might reach a breaking point and feel compelled to assert yourself. However, the damage may already be done by then, leaving you and your coworkers feeling hurt and confused.

You're not alone if you're seeking a way to navigate this situation more effectively. Learning to say no at work is a valuable skill that can help you maintain your sanity and productivity. Setting clear boundaries and respectfully declining tasks or requests that don't align with your goals is crucial for your mental health and professional satisfaction.

This guide will explore strategies for saying no assertively yet tactfully. Mastering this skill will reduce stress and frustration, foster healthier work relationships, and boost your overall well-being. Saying no isn't just about avoiding conflict; it's about prioritizing your needs and goals, ultimately benefiting everyone involved.

Why Saying No Is So Important

Saying no is about respect. Respect for oneself and others. When we say no, we declare our own boundaries, which indicates to ourselves and others that we have values and values, which are beliefs, goals, and limits we want to protect.

Saying no is a purposeful act. It empowers you because, by stating this is not what I want, you are effectively saying what you do want and thereby shaping your own life. If you can say no, you reclaim your power and agency by correctly balancing other people's interests, needs, and expectations against your own.

If you can say no in a healthy and conscious state of mind, you understand how to establish your own intention and steer your life in the direction you want it to go based on what is essential to you. The more you do this, the more confidence you will feel in your dreams and goals and your right to live your own life and do anything you want with it.

However, if you never say no, you end up conforming to other people's perceptions of who you are, what your life should be like, and what you should do. You prioritize others' needs, expectations, and comfort over your own. You suddenly find yourself doing everything you can to help them attain their goals while neglecting or discarding your own. As a result, your desires and opinions become less significant; your aspirations are unfulfilled; your boundaries are violated; and, in short, your life takes on a shape that is convenient for others rather than something you intended for yourself.

We don't only say no when something goes against our ideals. No is a useful word that helps us reduce stress and accept our own limitations. We cannot accomplish everything! Even if there are a lot of things you really want to say yes to, it requires maturity to focus on your priorities and say no when you are overwhelmed or have your mental and emotional resources stretched thin. Whether we like it or not, time and energy are always limited. We must budget them just like we do with our limited finances.

People place greater significance on your eyes when you say no forcefully and confidently. Rather than appearing to be a doormat who will do anything, people learn to appreciate your time and know that you will respect theirs by being straightforward about what you can and cannot do for them. When you value yourself, you convey it to others, which helps you avoid uncertainty, embarrassment, overwhelm, and guilt from saying yes when you shouldn't. You simply increase your own self-worth and add authenticity to your interactions. You don't take things personally or let guilt dictate your life.

Finally, one significant advantage of learning "no" is that it frees up time and energy to pursue what you truly care about—all those things to which you can answer a resounding yes!

Are you someone who is continually over-committing?

Many of us are taught to think of YES as a positive, helpful, and healthy word. However, this word can be extremely harmful. Perhaps your employer expects too much of you, so you work unpaid overtime or answer emails late at night when you should be relaxing. Maybe you find yourself performing all the housework or agreeing to handle all the planning for your social group. Perhaps you have a pushy family or a partner that you believe makes continual demands that you can't refuse. Between work commitments, children, family, studies, "life admin," and relationships, most of us have a lot of demands on our time, money, emotions, and even physical vitality.

Here's a fact about life: ***there will always be more to do than there is time to do it realistically.***

Knowing this, we can either adapt to our natural constraints or try and fail to do everything. Many people consistently say yes to everything and overcommit, feeling they are doing it to live a rich, fulfilling life, make others happy, solve problems, and so on. The truth, however, is that overcommitting harms everyone involved. The irony is that when we strive to do too much, we often end up doing very little. When we go out of our way to gain approval, we seem to get the least of it, and when we cross our own boundaries to make others happy, they appear to be the least happy of all.

Overcommitting typically results in a greater need for acceptance. You may have some of the personality qualities associated with overcommitting, such as being an ambitious "perfectionist" who prefers to be in control. But the negative is obvious: no matter how often we pretend to be superhuman, our energy eventually runs out, leaving us weary or with a few health concerns.

It's a painful irony that when we endeavor to be flawless, we are frequently forced to confront our limitations or, in extreme cases, fail. In an effort to impress others, we take on so much that we can't help but disappoint or let them down when we can't juggle as much as we thought we could. And when we seek the feeling of being almighty and capable of taking on everything, we can quickly become ill and exhausted, with our bodies virtually compelling us to stop and rest.

Chronic overcommitting (i.e., failing to say no when we should) has been related to poor sleep, an increased risk of heart disease and diabetes, and mood disorders such as anxiety or depression. When you are under strain, your body releases stress chemicals such as cortisol. While this surge usually helps you get through difficult or stressful moments, if the situation lasts too long, these hormones can induce inflammation in your body, inviting all kinds of diseases, not to mention weakening your immune system and resistance against stress in the future.

When we never say no, we never give up. We never rest. We never give our hearts, bodies, and brains time to heal and restore. When something is operated continually with no opportunity to recover, it develops wear and tear and eventually fails.

You could have headaches, allergies, strange aches and pains, exhaustion, irritation, digestive problems, or even unhealthy behaviors like overeating or substance addiction.

Burnout is nothing more than your body exhausting its physical, emotional, and mental resources. You may have been producing cortisol at such high levels for so long that your body is unable to do so anymore! The solution is not to take on more or add a new task to your To-do list, dubbed "fix burnout."

Rather, the goal is to find ways to pull back, rebuild ourselves, and achieve balance. And there's one magical word that can help us do so: "No."

But if this word is so fantastic, why don't we use it more?

Why Do We Struggle to Say No?

Granted, this would be a very short book if all it needed to improve your ability to say no was being told, "You should say no more." Most of us are aware that cognitively knowing the value of saying no and really saying no are two very different things. This is why it is critical to go deeply into the issue and understand why we are now struggling to establish appropriate boundaries and limit the demands on our time, energy, and emotions.

Consider the last time you refused to say no when you could (or should have!). Why haven't you said no? Perhaps you felt guilty.

But what are they guilty of? Where did the guilt come from, and what is it all about? This is what we will investigate in this chapter. There are numerous explanations for why we struggle to put our foot down. That is why it is critical to understand your specific reasons before contemplating any prospective answers. The effectiveness of any solution will be determined by how relevant it is to the problem we are currently facing.

You Want Others to Like You

Let us cut to the chase. Many of us say yes when we really mean no to project a certain image. We agree to extra labor to appear focused and committed to our employment. We agree to help at the food bank to appear unselfish and community-minded. We even agree to go on the second date to appear easygoing and friendly.

Nobody loves a damp blanket who disappoints the team, right? So you say yes even though you don't want to. Maybe you want to appear busy and in demand. Perhaps you're flattered that your attention and efforts are necessary, and you enjoy being sought out in this way. Of course, having the freedom to do things your way rather than relying on others is a benefit.

When we look further, however, we discover that this rationale is nothing more than the need for others to like us. We visualize ourselves as the person we want to be and act accordingly: nice, accommodating, helpful, and hardworking. We believe we will get greater respect and popularity by agreeing to and assisting them with their demands.

Humans are social beings, and this is an instinct, but it can spiral out of control in those who overcommit.

If You Say No, You're Afraid of Missing Out on Anything

Sometimes, we say yes because we want to be the well-liked individuals who, we believe, say yes. Sometimes, we simply say yes because we are terrified of what will happen if we don't. Our supervisor may present us with a stressful opportunity that will not be available again if we decline it now. Perhaps we are concerned that saying no would hurt our prospects or make us less in demand if clients regard us as untrustworthy or unwilling to help.

This also applies to personal interactions. How many people have committed to each other because they believed that they would lose their spouse unless they showed some willingness to endanger the relationship? Friends, family, or romantic partners may transmit to us an implicit rule: if we say no, all hell breaks loose. We bend ourselves out of shape to avoid losing them or making them unhappy.

Finally, we may say yes not because we truly mean it but because we have the dreaded FOMO—Fear of Missing Out. We imagine everyone else living life to the fullest and that if we don't say yes, we pass up opportunities for happiness. When you think about it, the pressure is great!

You Genuinely Care

Parents can become exhausted from always saying yes because they sincerely care about their children and want the best for them. They prioritize their children's happiness over their own. Consider someone who quits their work to become a full-time caregiver for a sick spouse or who agrees to get up in the middle of the night to assist with an animal shelter emergency.

Of course, there is nothing wrong with wanting to help, do good in the world, care for those we love, or strive to make a positive influence in the lives of others. It's good to observe and attempt to alleviate suffering in the world. If we believe that saying no will injure someone we care about, we are more likely to say yes.

You Feel You Must Care

Finally, consider the most common reason for overcommitment: the belief that saying no is simply not acceptable. This is significantly different from the other reasons—we may agree to something because we actually want to do it or because we desire the effect it will have (i.e., we will be liked), but many of us say yes merely because we feel obligated to.

What is the meaning behind this "should"? Our beliefs, values, and principles guide everything we do, and they stem not only from ourselves but also from our family experiences and cultural programming. We may have an unquestioned story that states, for example, "When someone offers you food, you say yes no matter what." This is not always benevolence but rather a knowledge of obligation, convention, and civility.

There's a little of the reason two mixed in here—we may be afraid that if we don't say yes, we'll have to deal with the unpleasant consequences of feeling awful, such as guilt. This shame demonstrates a conflict between our genuine goals and constraints and their misalignment with what we believe we should feel and do. When we feel guilty, we can presume that we have broken a value or principle, whether it is our own or one imposed on us by others. We may feel guilty because we expect "payback," which could be self-judgment or the condemnation of others.

In fact, persons who have developed the practice of saying yes when they mean no may eventually lose touch with their true thoughts and feelings. These are the ones who don't even consider saying no; it doesn't occur to them. Such a person may be dissatisfied for no apparent reason, or they may uncover the true source of the stress much later.

As you can see, numerous answers exist to why we find it difficult to say no. However, they can all be explained by a single overarching theme: *codependency*.

All the causes above boil down to our specific conversations with people on the border of self and others. In a shared world, there is always a trade-off between our own wants and limitations and those of others. It is up to us to decide where we will draw that line.

Some people are very selfish, taking more than they give and prioritizing their own needs to the detriment of others.

"People pleasers" have the opposite imbalance—they give more than they take and prioritize others' needs over their own. If you are a people-pleaser, you may have experienced all four of the causes above in your life. You may struggle with saying no and asking for help, expressing your needs, or admitting that you are struggling. You may despise conflict and go to great lengths to please others. You may find yourself doing things independently because it is easier, and you may not want to risk losing your relationships.

You don't want to offend, disappoint, or be criticized, so you say yes before even considering what you're being asked (and may subsequently feel resentful). Sometimes, you feel as if someone has a "hold" on you. Being viewed as nice and helpful boosts your self-esteem, yet you are extremely concerned about saying no, preferring to say yes and deal with the consequences alone.

The codependency part comes in when you need people to approve of you; in other words, you need to be needed. You may sacrifice yourself but believe that they are not appreciative enough, and you unconsciously hold this against others, reassured that they cannot abandon you because you have helped them so much and been so beneficial. The end outcome of constantly saying yes is surprisingly negative: you may feel trapped, taken advantage of, worthless, torn, overloaded, and frustrated with yourself for being a doormat! You might have been taught to be considerate, kind, and helpful, but you still feel deeply uncared for.

The Psychological Root of Never Saying No: Codependency.

Let us take a closer look at the codependency dynamic.

Codependency, originally defined in psychology as the connections that grow around someone with an addiction, is today viewed as a web of psychological patterns in which one person takes too little responsibility for issues while another takes too much. Codependency extends beyond being polite and helpful. When we are codependent, we become engrossed in other people's needs, believing that we are personally responsible for their feelings and that it is our exclusive responsibility to fix their issues and make them happy.

While empathetic aid is one thing, codependency may lead to enabling and playing the rescuer for others, disempowering them and increasing their reliance on you over time. Without correct limits and the ability to say no, you create a relationship based on obligation, entitlement, dependency, and misdirected responsibilities. Codependency is unpleasant for both parties, but you're probably the overcommitted and over-responsible member of the dynamic if you're reading this.

Codependency can be difficult to see in ourselves because we prefer to believe that we are acting rationally or doing what is best for the other person. We could lack a clear and honest grasp of our own motivations. However, suppose you are continually uncomfortable with the demands and expectations placed on you. In that case, if you are literally unable to say no, if you have anxiety or fuzzy boundaries in your relationships, or if you frequently feel taken for granted, codependency may be an issue for you.

It's important to understand the essential underlying idea at the heart of codependency. This core belief is that I can affect another person's emotions. To put it another way, I am accountable for another person's emotions.

We may contrast this with a healthier form of compassion that states, "I can always love, empathize with, and support others, but I cannot live their lives for them." When we have healthy boundaries, we know which feelings are ours or someone else's. We understand that we can control our own behavior but not others. We understand that we are responsible for ourselves and that others bear their own duty. When we exhibit codependence, however, we become entangled with other people in ways that are detrimental to both.

A typical example is a wife whose husband drinks. Assume he becomes really drunk and then lashes out, smashes stuff, and threatens everyone, including her. When he gets sober, he either denies whatever happened, blames her, or says that she should have done more to stop him. One day, he is caught on drunk and disorderly charges, and he requests that she bail him out of jail with all of her savings. She can't say no. Who else will save him? She makes allowances for his poor behavior, unconsciously loving that she is his sole defender and helper.

He takes no responsibility for his behavior; however, she accepts full responsibility, assuring him on the way home that she will work more to reduce tension at home so he is not tempted to drink. A few days later, he asks her to buy a few bottles of wine, and she can't say no. The cycle begins anew. She tells others that he makes her life miserable, but the truth is that she has never considered leaving him and, in an unhealthy manner, enjoys being the moral savior. Doesn't she enjoy feeling so needed?

While this is an extreme case, we've all been guilty of the same dynamic at some point. We may play the long-suffering martyr or assume feelings or concerns that are not solely our responsibility. The problem with codependency is that it simply does not work. We can't save others from the repercussions of their choices, we can't make someone feel something, and we can't live anyone else's life.

We may enter into this type of relationship pattern for numerous reasons.

What about the big one? *Fear.*

What exactly are you afraid of? Of rejection, displeasure, or fury. Fear of losing control and suffering a dreadful outcome. We may be afraid of losing a relationship, receiving judgment from others, or simply not wanting to confront an uncomfortable or unpleasant truth.

Consistently saying yes can serve as a protective shell, reducing insecurities and increasing control.

When your inner self-esteem is unstable, you are more inclined to crave external acceptance. You may need to feel useful, helpful, and necessary to feel worthwhile as a person, or you may believe that if you do not bend over backward, you will lose what is vital to you. So, instead of reaching out to loved ones with compassion and genuine care, we do so out of guilt, shame, and fear.

A parent may never be confident to set financial restrictions with his adult children because he fears losing their love. This is because, deep down, he lacks confidence and security in himself outside his ability to produce money. A woman may continuously agree to cook for family holidays despite the burden because she feels judged by her husband's family, who prefers his former wife. She feels pressured to agree to whatever they ask so that she is not compared poorly to her ex.

Misplaced trust is another major cause of codependent behavior. This means that we incorrectly assign others the role of providing our lives meaning, purpose, and value when it is actually our responsibility. Of course, humans will always have some level of attachment and dependence on other humans, which is normal and good.

However, when we let other people's behaviors, feelings, and thoughts define us, we lose our autonomy. It is acceptable to trust and submit to others within certain limits, but when we are codependent, we almost trust too much, relying on others to cover voids in ourselves. Some codependent relationships have a transactional element, as in "if you take care of me this way, I'll take care of you that way, and we'll be together forever because we both can't live without the other."

With awareness, we may reclaim healthy responsibility for ourselves while gradually learning to say no to tasks that are not our responsibility. And it is worth it!

Codependency is really detrimental to us. Codependency destroys relationships and individuals rather than strengthening them.

It causes hatred. People do not recognize or reciprocate your efforts; you feel taken for granted. Anger and entitlement simmer inside you because you choose to give too much. Perhaps you offer even more in the hopes of being noticed and rewarded. However, resentment can fester and eventually explode, or it can lead to passive-aggressive or grumbling behavior.

It causes physical and mental problems. We've already witnessed the significant health costs associated with chronic stress and overcommitting. Depression and anxiety are nearly inevitable, which means you are working extremely hard and going out of your way to make yourself unhappy.

It causes emotional and spiritual problems. Disconnecting from your own wants and limitations causes misery and ruins your inner sense of worth and purpose. Unresolved issues of guilt, self-worth, and fear will continue to influence and jeopardize your life unless you work them out intentionally.

It does not even work! Is all this turmoil and grief really worth it? No. The people we strive to pacify, impress, or mend never seem to respond with praise and thanks, and their circumstances do not mysteriously improve when we take from ourselves to give to them. It's tempting to believe that all of this sacrifice and self-denial is a big and noble price to pay—but this is a fallacy. The best and healthiest relationships are those in which people love one another while simultaneously loving themselves.

BUILD YOUR "NO" MUSCLE

After years of being a "yes man," saying "no" might seem awkward and unpleasant. As you practice the tasks from the previous chapter, you may find them simpler but still tough. Speaking up and asserting boundaries can lead to more respect and confidence, making it simpler to do so in the future.

We need to exercise our no muscles on a regular basis to keep them healthy and robust, just as we do with our muscles to train and strengthen them. Initially, the task may appear difficult. Trying a high-intensity workout for the first time can be challenging, like a lifetime couch potato attempting a new activity. Learning to say no is analogous to improving one's fitness: it becomes easier with practice.

If you're struggling with changing your thinking, remember that it won't last forever. Over time, your attitude, self-concept, and ability to maintain appropriate limits will improve. If practiced consistently, saying no at the correct time can become an effortless habit.

Saying yes all the time is a negative habit, but learning to say no is a good one to practice. Before we get into the practical nuts and bolts of expressing yourself (similar to the physical exercises you'd do to build a certain muscle), we'll go over the many types of assertiveness.

Assertiveness

People who struggle with saying no often equate the word with rudeness, aggressiveness, or stubbornness. The word "no" is often associated with tantrums or being tough. To learn assertiveness, it's important to understand the various colors and nuances of the word "no," which is used to set boundaries.

A basic assertion is simply a statement of necessity, choice, limit, or personal view. For example, "My budget for this is $500."

"I'm not happy with the service I've received."

"I'm celiac and can't eat that."

"I'm really upset right now."

Basic claims occur when we state facts or express ourselves within our rights. Maintaining simplicity and neutrality is key to effectively communicating basic assertions. We do not need to beg, plead, explain, justify, or apologize. It doesn't only have to be factual. When expressing our feelings, utilize "I" words to own them. For example, "I don't think this looks good," rather than "this is hideous." Accepting responsibility for one's emotions, beliefs, desires, and limitations may be extremely empowering. It can be difficult to speak up and make these issues known.

For example, if someone keeps offering you food, simply reply, "Thank you, but I'm watching my weight and don't want any more."

A clever method to indirectly express a basic statement is to ask, "What would you like me to deprioritize?" For example, when your supervisor assigns you additional tasks, this conveys the message: "I can only do so many things at once—which ones should they be?" Set boundaries without being rigid and delegate responsibility for resolving overload to others.

An empathic assertion considers the other person's feelings, needs, and wants while expressing your own. Mastering the "saying no means I don't care" mindset is crucial. Using empathetic assertions communicates to the other person that you are stating your boundaries while also acknowledging and being sensitive to their perspective.

"I understand that you were expecting a better conclusion. I'm afraid this is the outcome for now."

"I understand that you are overwhelmed by this project. I must, however, request that you direct these issues to the appropriate channels from now on."

"I am sure you haven't had it easy lately. As we discussed, I still require you to carry out your tasks on this project."

This type of assertion has a wide range of applications. We can use it to request extra support and thoughtfulness or to decline requests when we are unable to provide them. While saying no and setting boundaries may cause trouble or disappointment, it's important to demonstrate regret and compassion nonetheless.

Notice that in the above phrases, we avoid following the empathic comment with "but," which would just wipe out any feelings of compassion and come out as passive-aggressive. For instance, saying, "I see your point, but..." may appear disingenuous or dismissive. Instead, try using "and" or softening your phrases to avoid diminishing the empathy you're communicating.

Hopefully, you won't have to make many consequence assertions.

Setting and communicating appropriate boundaries and asserting them when others threaten to overstep can reduce the need for such assertions. When someone crosses our boundaries or is aggressive, it's important to reply appropriately without being confrontational.

19

The goal is to avoid hostility and strong emotions. Maintain a quiet voice, neutral tone, and relaxed body language. Remember that a boundary is a type of conditional statement, such as "If X, then Y." To claim this is not to issue a threat or ultimatum but rather to state a fact.

"If you talk to me like that again, I'm going to end the conversation and take some time to reconsider this relationship."

"I'm afraid I'm not willing to keep participating in this project until the safety concerns raised are properly addressed."

"If this behavior doesn't change, I will have no choice but to get your supervisor involved."

Consequence assertions are used as a final option after ignoring benign boundary assertions. Enforcing a boundary with genuine consequences is crucial for its effectiveness.

Delivering an "ultimatum" can be challenging but can also empower you. Do not make such an assumption unless you have actual repercussions to deliver and are sincerely determined to follow through on them.

A discrepancy assertion may be required prior to a consequence assertion. This is merely you pointing out the discrepancy between what was agreed upon and what is actually happening, indicating a misunderstanding, contradiction, or broken promise.

"We agreed last week that I would have the final say on the budget, but now you want a second opinion on the figures." Can you confirm that this is what we agreed?

"When we signed up for that marathon, you promised me you'd train with me every other day, rain or shine, remember?"

A discrepancy assertion gives the opposing party time to follow the agreement or back off a boundary. It reminds them that it exists and will not be pushed back gradually.

Use negative feelings declarations to convey how someone's action affects you emotionally. This is not to blame them or hold them accountable but to make them aware of their impact on you and allow them the opportunity to change. Begin by explaining their conduct as honestly and gently as possible, and then clearly explain how it affects you without making broad generalizations or judgments. Begin with expressing your emotions, followed by your desired action.

Don't say, "You never sleep when you should, keep me awake all night, and make me foggy in the morning. It sucks."

Say, "Coming to bed late makes it harder for me to sleep. I often feel fatigued in the mornings. I would appreciate it if you could commit to coming to bed on time in the future, as agreed.

While practicing the following, keep in mind that you may need to repeat yourself. Try the "broken record" technique, which involves repeating yourself quietly and neutrally over and over. It's important to do this since those who want to push your boundaries will frequently do so gradually, thinking that your no will eventually become a yes.

Mentally Preparing Yourself

If you struggle with saying no, you may say "yes" without fully considering the situation. Requests can take you off guard, leading to an automatic "yes" response without thought. It's important to be prepared to say no, as it can be difficult to maintain focus and strength in stressful situations.

Don't get into the trap of automatically saying yes unless you've developed the confidence to say no. Saying no is simpler when you're prepared. Prepare a rationale for saying no. It's not necessary to provide a strong reason for your refusal to comply with the request. You have the right to say "no" if you don't want to say yes. Having a clear and concise rationale for saying no can help you remain calm and confident.

If you have your own personal code of values and beliefs, it can make things easier by eliminating the need to reinvent the wheel with each request, deciding whether to answer yes or no right away. "I'm sorry, but I can't do that. I do not work on weekends. There's no agonizing or debating—you simply do not work on weekends. It is a rule, end of story. You can respond quickly because you are aware of your schedule and lifestyle. This lifestyle acts as a boundary, requiring you to communicate frequently. If you know what your schedule is ("I don't have time on Wednesdays"), your limits ("I don't drink more than two drinks in an evening"), and your requirements ("I need my quiet time in the mornings"), you are essentially prepared to answer when someone asks you to step outside of these parameters.

If you are a chronic people-pleaser or frequently say yes because you want others to approve of you, you may feel compelled to respond to a request right away. If you have some time to think about it, you can always say, "I'm not sure—can I get back to you on that?" We may be accustomed to feeling uncertain yet saying yes, but we must train ourselves to view uncertainty as a hint that we should take our time before committing to anything.

Ask yourself if you truly want to do anything.

What value does it provide to your life, and how much does it cost? You may be able to comply, but does that imply you should? Are you tempted to say yes because you really want to do it or for another reason?

Changing Your Behaviors and Beliefs, One No at a Time

Once you've prepared yourself in this way and established your boundaries, routines, wants, preferences, and "rules," you can say no. If you have properly prepared and worked on the underlying blockages that make saying no tough, this stage should be much easier than you think.

Remember that you always have the right to say no, and you're not doing anything wrong. If you say no to someone, you are rejecting their request, not them as a person. We are free to make decisions based on what we value—we may accept other people's refusals and assert our right to say no to others.

Will some people resent you for saying no? Of course. But how will you handle their reaction? The truth is that you don't need to do anything. This is their reaction.

You can be kind and sensitive to their feelings but do not have to change yourself to meet their disappointment. You may discover that the contrary is true—that people are perfectly eager to accept a no if only you gave them one and that they are more resilient and capable than you may have given them credit for. A funny side effect of learning to say no is understanding you've been bending over backward when other people have always been perfectly capable of doing without it!

Be prepared to make mistakes when practicing saying no. You want to be direct, unbiased, and honest without being cold or harsh. For example, you don't have to justify, explain, apologize, or plead, but it doesn't mean you can't be courteous.

A bit rude: "Nope. "I can't do it."

More courteous yet effective: "I appreciate you contacting me to inquire.

I'm afraid I can't assist you with that this time. Could you ask so-and-so?

It may be tempting at first to talk a lot, explain, or justify, but it is nearly always preferable to keep things brief and straightforward. The longer you blabber on, the less assured you will feel and the more dishonest you risk appearing.

Use a kind tone of voice, open body language, and a smile when appropriate. Speak slowly, and take your time. To demonstrate honesty and genuineness, confessing difficulty with a request or needing time to consider your response is acceptable. Do relaxing breathing exercises or unclench your jaw and knuckles to avoid transmitting nervousness or doubt during critical conversations. Nonverbal communication is equally vital as verbal communication.

Use the phrase "I don't want to" instead of "I can't" or making excuses or blaming others. When people hear you say "I can't" when you actually mean "I won't," they may take it as insincerity or evasion. You'll respect yourself more and acquire the respect of others if you can peacefully accept responsibility for yourself. Consider things from the opposite side. If you asked a friend to a gathering, would you prefer to say, "I'm sorry, but I'm unable to attend tonight." I promised my grandmother I would walk her dog, and there is no way I can get out of it! "I'm sorry, but I'm not feeling up to socializing tonight. Also, I think I'm coming down with something." "I'm going to spend a quiet night in."

One major advantage of being honest, transparent, and polite is that your example will motivate others to follow suit. They can be confident in saying no to you without making excuses or saying yes when they don't want to. Inadvertently, you build a more true, honest connection. It may seem like a good idea to go along with things or say yes to keep the peace.

However, keep in mind the long-term costs of this strategy: resentment, disappointment, bitterness, and the sensation of doing things for others out of obligation rather than want. Don't you think your relationships deserve better?

Saying No Strategically and in the Right Tone

So far, we've examined in depth why we struggle to say no and how to rewrite our attitudes and core beliefs to adopt the attitude of someone with tighter, healthier boundaries. Even if you're confident and aggressive, opening your mouth and saying something might be challenging for many. When someone makes a request, their willpower fades, and they struggle to answer no as planned.

What matters most is your attitude. Nothing beats a healthy, balanced, and confident mindset. However, this does not imply that tone of voice is irrelevant.

It doesn't mean we shouldn't think about our word choice, posture, and body language. In other words, while we have the right to express our limits and say no, learning to be nice is also a valuable skill!

As a human being, you naturally consider the impact of your actions and words on others. Even if you don't prioritize acceptance, you still want to be liked and help others. In this section, we want to strike a balance between strength and softness, assertiveness and compassion. We all want to believe that we are rational, fair, and balanced, whether we say yes or no—and tone of voice helps us do so.

To effectively say no, follow these guidelines:

- Be clear
- Be firm
- No excuses.

We'll keep the aforementioned in mind throughout. Your personal boundaries are your top priority. After that, you can adjust your tone to be pleasant, reasonable, and accommodating.

In fact, you may discover that being firm and unambiguous and refusing to make numerous explanations makes it simpler to be nice and polite. Once you've stated your position unequivocally, it's as if you're just two friends attempting to negotiate around an immovable reality, such as the weather or today is Thursday. After accepting a solid no, it's easier to go on.

No means no. However, here are some strategies you can use to make your no go down easier and be heard by others. First, remain cool. This is the most crucial. When others request us, it can feel like we're put on the spot and expected to respond quickly. However, this feeling of pressure will simply put you on the back foot, making you reactive rather than proactive.

So do not rush. Pause to allow for processing. You have the freedom! Take your time with requests, as they are already asking for something from you. You are not required to react immediately. To calm yourself down when feeling flustered, try saying, "I don't know, let me think about it and then I'll get back to you." This approach is straightforward and avoids creating unbreakable obligations.

Examine your schedule, money, and energy levels. Inquire about the cost and benefits of saying yes. Check within yourself to discover if you're eager to say yes for the wrong reasons. Then, on your own time and on your own terms, plan your response and be ready to give it. Doing things this way immediately increases your control and calms you down. Our tension stems from the belief that we are only valuable or likable if we are swift and efficient, which perpetuates the counter-mindset. However, your time and energy are finite and hence important; communicate this to others by being careful with how you spend them!

If you want to say no without being unpleasant or inconvenient, a good strategy is to say yes to something else. This approach is viewed as accommodating as it addresses both your and their demands. Let's say your sister asks you to look after her children over the weekend. You say I'm sorry, but I can't this weekend. But I can phone a reliable babysitter I know and see if she is available."

You comply on your own terms and make an offer that is likely to be accepted rather than rejected. In fact, if you apply this strategy correctly, people may be tempted to thank you and express gratitude after you decline. It's a win-win!

However, to respond in this manner requires practice and preparation. Don't just practice the words you'll say; setting boundaries and expressing no entails so much more than just saying "no."

- You need to practice remaining calm.
- You should use a forceful, confident tone of voice.
- You need to maintain a calm body posture.
- You should practice being clear, concise, and minimalist.

If someone says, "Uhhh, no," in a weak and scared tone, accompanied by apologetic nonverbal communication and a plethora of justifications, it isn't truly a no. However, even if you don't use "no," your intention and message are clearly communicated. We've learned that no is more than simply a word; it's a way of thinking. When you display calm, uncomplicated, and confident assertiveness, others will undoubtedly mirror your behavior. What matters most is that you believe you have the right to say no and are unwavering and confident in doing so. If you feel this way, you can express it to others.

Practice saying no and then being quiet. Don't be afraid to fill silences after you've stated what you need to say. Say, I'm sorry, but I can't do that." Then stop speaking. Allow the other person to hear and comprehend what you have spoken. Do not "protest too much" by softening your own statement as soon as you express it.

Use courteous language such as "I appreciate you asking, but.." "I wish I could, but unfortunately, that won't work this time . . "

Avoid using these polite expressions if you think you'll get carried away with explaining, justifying, and making explanations. You are not "sorry" when you say, "I'm sorry, but no." You are simply being courteous and accepting that they may be disappointed with your refusal.

Similarly, it's acceptable to refer to someone else's decision that prevents you from saying yes (I'd love to, but my doctor told me I shouldn't travel for a few days"), but be careful: you want to make it appear as if it's ultimately your decision to defer to this other person. Consider the difference between: "Sorry, I can't go." The babysitter canceled, so I had to stay at home tonight. "I'd love to, but Wednesday is dinner with the family, and I promised myself never to miss those!"

It's a subtle distinction. However, if you don't want your no to come across as a lame excuse, make it a point to emphasize that you still chose to say no based on your own agency rather than passively blaming something outside your control. It can be tempting to believe that if we point out something beyond our control, the other person will understand and forgive us, but the contrary is often true.

When we choose not to do something instead of saying we can't, we appear more confident and in charge. Furthermore, you don't want to make an excuse only to have the other person remove it for you, believing you'll naturally say okay ("No worries!"). We know a sitter. I'll phone her so she can come over. Problem solved!").

If you are a chronic people-pleaser, you may have the habit of believing you are being "polite" while, in reality, you are being a pushover or unclear. We express remorse or say, "I'm sorry," and our no fades or becomes a yes somehow. How can we distinguish between over-explaining or making excuses and being respectful? How do we distinguish between language that says, "I'm a pushover; don't take me seriously," and language that is reasonable, flexible, and professional?

So, we return to our golden rules:

- Be clear
- Be firm
- No excuses.

If we are straightforward, we will avoid being misinterpreted. If we expressly say no, we can use politeness as a nice addition rather than replacing or undermining the no. Here's an example: "I'd love to, and you know I enjoy our nights out, but this time it's a no from me." Use the broken record approach to keep repeating yourself without contributing anything new."I know you were looking forward to it, but not tonight."

If you are firm, there is nothing left to say, nothing to negotiate, and nothing to back down. Consider yourself a steadfast yet friendly rock. Be polite and show concern for others, and avoid making excuses. However, this does not diminish the importance of our own perspective. As long as you are strong and clear and avoid making excuses, you can be as polite, kind, professional, and accommodating as you like.

This requires talent and a significant mentality shift—we must teach ourselves and others that we are a cooperative, nice, kind team member who cares while remaining strong within our bounds. When you understand how this is done, you know it's never about balancing people's approval with your boundaries.

You can have both.

Consider these courteous statements that effectively establish a clear limit without resorting to excuses: "I'm flattered you've asked me to be your best man, and I'm ecstatic you're getting married. But, to be honest, I don't think I could spend the time required, and you deserve a more available best man. Melissa and I will be your guests. (No excuses. Instead, a smaller, more humane commitment was made. "Sorry, it's just not a good time right now." (Note that you do not need to rush in and commit to when a "good time" might be, but you are not ruling out the idea of saying yes later.

"Actually, I've made other commitments, so it's going to have to be a no from me this time." (Again, "this time" lessens the impact while maintaining the firmness of the no right now.) "Well, if I figure out how to clone myself, then maybe, but I just don't have the availability this time" (Using comedy to reduce awkwardness while demonstrating the impossibility of dispute, i.e., remaining firm.) "Unfortunately/sadly, that won't work for me" (This is a simple acceptance of the potential disappointment that may arise from the no.) "Thank you for the offer, but no. Perhaps next time? "I'm on a tight budget this month and won't be spending a lot on Christmas gifts."

Many assertiveness self-help books will focus on what to say and how to say it, but as you can see, it's more vital to first get your thinking right, be clear, cool, and excuse-free... and then communicate. How you convey your limits will differ based on who you speak with, the setting, and why. There is no universally effective approach to saying no. However, if you can manage to overcome counter-mindsets and stay focused on what is important, you will gradually improve your natural assertiveness. If you are clear about your boundaries and have the correct mindset, you may change the surface details to suit each new situation.

Buy Yourself Time

You've seen how to mentally prepare so that you can answer requests with calm confidence.

You've (hopefully) begun to change your beliefs, attitudes, and behaviors one at a time.

You've noticed that exercising your no-muscle is frequently more about how you say things than what you say.

As you do all of this, remember that it will take time for you to feel more at ease putting your foot down. People may be surprised or uncomfortable with your new attitude, especially if they previously loved you being a doormat! However, one strategy we can always employ to improve our skills is to purchase time.

Another way to look at it is to try to be less reactive overall.

People-pleasers are especially sensitive to the demands of a 24/7, always-on society that teaches you to respond, react, and comply swiftly and consistently. When you're overwhelmed, saying "I'll get back to yo" is a clever ploy, but it's better to cultivate deeper resilience and avoid overreacting in the long run.

Being reactive involves allowing external events to influence one's emotions and behaviors rather than being motivated by one's own desires and choices.

We are all connected to our surroundings and people, yet relying only on their actions and words might lead to reactivity. Reactive individuals tend to blame others, seek praise, and adjust their moods based on external factors.

You feel like a balloon being tossed around in heavy winds. When your employer yells, you despair. When your child throws a tantrum, you drop everything and run to deal with it. When you receive an email notice, you tend to focus solely on replying to it, losing track of your previous task. And if the email contains negative news, your mood immediately deteriorates, even if you were joyful just before.

You are reacting to life rather than intentionally selecting how to move through it. You are completely in fight-or-flight mode, talking and doing without considering what you're doing or why. You tend to let others and situations rule you without considering how you may take control. A related concept is your locus of control, or where you see the power and control in your life coming from. Does your life move forward due to external circumstances, or do you drive it?

Being proactive does not imply that everything goes your way; rather, it means that you are present, conscious, and able to choose how to respond to life. How might we cultivate this mental clarity? Well, mindfulness is an obvious path. When we pause to become aware of ourselves in the moment, we create space between ourselves and events as they unfold, allowing us to insert our own will, intention, and desire. Taking a pause allows us to focus on our own feelings, needs, and desires rather than external expectations or others'.

Being attentive allows us to disconnect from powerful, instinctive emotions and respond more thoughtfully. We can control our reactions and prevent them from becoming overwhelming. We instantly gain more control and awareness in a circumstance. We can choose how strongly we want to react to anything or whether we want to respond at all. We may pick what to concentrate on rather than having things demand our attention. And, with awareness, we can make an essential decision: say no if we want to!

So, buying yourself time and delaying your response is a byproduct of being proactive, mindful, and having an internal rather than external locus of control. Mindset and locus of control are inextricably linked. Consider the following. "My supervisor is upset because I failed to complete all reports by Friday, despite our agreement. He has unrealistic expectations of me and should not have requested so much from me. I'm already overworked, and he never respects how hard I work. I'm treated poorly at work, and I don't deserve it. That's why I'm always anxious and miserable. "I told my employer

I could finish the reports by Friday, but I couldn't, and he's understandably upset. I was obligated to temper his expectations and inform him I needed more time rather than simply saying yes. My boss appreciates me, yet he cannot read my mind and expects me to keep my word. It's my responsibility to manage my workload, and I'll be more attentive to avoid setting myself up for failure in the future.

The first one is undoubtedly easier. However, the second option is considerably more likely to result in honest improvement and calmer control in the future. Your self-esteem, identity, work ethic, ideals, and relationships with others will all benefit if you can take conscious ownership of what is truly under your control.

Accept responsibility for your feelings and behaviors.

To increase mindfulness in your dealings with others, halt and count to three when someone makes a request. Do not worry about awkward silence. If you're feeling rushed and uncomfortable, say something like, "I'll get back to you," or, "Let me check my calendar." Consider your calendar or lifestyle "rules," and if necessary, express your availability, such as "Unfortunately, I'm not available on Thursday evenings." Then stop speaking! Remember to be cool and clear and prevent making excuses. If you feel comfortable, use some comedy.

If you use email, you can even consider setting up an automated answer when you are unavailable so it can say no on your behalf. You could provide an option or place the person in the direction of someone who can assist.

HOW TO SAY NO TO YOUR BOSS

In the modern workplace, the dynamics between employees and their supervisors are pivotal in shaping both individual success and organizational effectiveness. At the heart of this relationship lies the concept of boundaries—limits and expectations that define how individuals interact, collaborate, and navigate their professional responsibilities.

Setting boundaries with your boss isn't just about asserting your independence or protecting personal time; it's a strategic maneuver essential for career growth and well-being. Consider this: clear boundaries establish mutual respect and delineate roles and responsibilities, ensuring that tasks are delegated effectively and executed efficiently. Without boundaries, the lines between work and personal life blur, leading to burnout, resentment, and diminished performance.

Moreover, boundaries foster open communication and trust within the workplace. When employees feel empowered to express their needs and preferences, it cultivates a culture of transparency and accountability. This, in turn, enhances collaboration and problem-solving, as teams can navigate challenges with clarity and cohesion.

It's good to know that acknowledging the necessity of setting boundaries with your boss doesn't discount the inherent power dynamic at play. Feeling apprehensive about asserting yourself is natural, especially when it involves pushing back against authority. However, embracing this discomfort is the first step towards reclaiming agency and autonomy in your professional life.

Remember, boundaries aren't about erecting barriers or challenging authority for its own sake; they're about fostering a healthy and productive work environment. By establishing clear expectations and respectfully asserting your needs, you're advocating for yourself and contributing to a culture of mutual respect and collaboration.

As we delve deeper, we'll explore practical strategies and actionable insights to help you navigate challenging conversations and assert your boundaries effectively. From crafting assertive messages to handling pushback and overcoming common obstacles, you'll gain the tools and confidence needed to navigate the complexities of the employee-boss relationship with grace and resilience.

Understanding the Importance

In any workplace, the relationship between an employee and their boss is a cornerstone of professional life. This dynamic can significantly impact job satisfaction, productivity, and overall career trajectory. However, within this relationship, it's essential to recognize the pivotal role of boundaries.

Boundaries serve as the framework for healthy interactions and effective collaboration. They delineate expectations, responsibilities, and acceptable behaviors, helping to create a respectful and harmonious work environment. Without clear boundaries, misunderstandings can arise, leading to conflicts, inefficiencies, and even resentment.

One of the primary reasons why setting boundaries with your boss is crucial is to preserve work-life balance. The line between professional obligations and personal time can easily blur in today's fast-paced work culture. Without boundaries in place, employees may find themselves constantly fielding work-related requests outside of office hours, leading to burnout and diminished well-being.

Moreover, boundaries are essential for fostering mutual respect and trust within the workplace. When employees feel empowered to assert their needs and limitations, it cultivates a culture of openness and collaboration. Conversely, a lack of boundaries can erode trust and breed resentment, as employees may feel taken advantage of or undervalued.

From a career development perspective, setting boundaries with your boss is also crucial for establishing your professional identity and asserting your organizational values. By communicating your boundaries effectively, you demonstrate confidence, assertiveness, and self-awareness—highly valued qualities in the workplace. This, in turn, can lead to increased opportunities for growth, recognition, and advancement.

Boundaries with Your Boss

If you read a review of yourself, you may be described as "accommodating" and "agreeable." While this may be a positive appraisal at work, are these appropriate words to describe the situation in general? Be cautious since the mistaken positivism around them may mislead you.

Being accommodating or agreeable does not involve imposing limits but rather adapting to keep others happy. This lacks assertiveness.

It's not wrong to be nice, and it often stems from empathy—a psychological drive to promote social harmony and improve the lives of others. It has a beneficial effect on its own and is neutral at worst. Blurring boundaries for the sake of being pleasant can have a negative impact on life.

Agreeableness can stem from a desire to be liked, which can lead to self-suppression and a loss of authenticity. Most people dislike people-pleasing, highlighting the complexities of human nature.

In a 2010 study published in the Journal of Personality and Social Psychology, researchers compared people's responses to selfish and selfless actions in a prize game. The study indicated that generous players were disliked almost as much as selfish ones.

Members who contributed to a public good but only used a small portion was expelled from the group. Two follow-up investigations confirmed that the observed outcomes were not due to unpredictability or confusion. People disliked both generous and selfish athletes equally.

These affable players seemed to make others feel horrible about themselves. They were also considered "rule-breakers." They were positively breaking unfavorable societal conventions, but it was excessive. Excessive politeness, whether motivated by admiration or social harmony, can lead to exclusion from the intended group.

You may have attempted to gain favor with a group by taking on unpopular tasks or paying for drinks at a work event. Excessive giving can make people uncomfortable, much like selfish behavior that makes life difficult or prevents contribution.

Opposing the norm, even by good deeds, might make you a target. You may be suggested for voluntary redundancy or find it challenging to obtain a seat in a car during a road trip, just like a selfish individual.

In 2011, researchers at the University of Notre Dame discovered that employees who disagreed earned more than those who agreed. Disagreeable men earned 18% more than agreeable men. Although agreeableness is a socially anticipated trait in women, disagreeable women earned 5% more than pleasant women and fared poorly compared to disagreeable men.

Agreeable people avoid difficult topics, such as wage hikes or higher starting salaries. Agreeing on everything is a sure way to become a pushover.

The amiable employee has a heavy task that keeps him awake at night. He agreed to assist five coworkers who sought him for help. They've spoken about what he does all day and whether he has time to help everyone.

He accepts his boss's outrageous demands, concealing his approaching gloom about how he will complete the tasks.

When a colleague refuses to help others, he demands higher pay and promotion to a managerial position due to frequent requests for advice. The supervisor delegated some of his workload to an affable employee.

Throughout childhood, individuals are taught to prioritize kindness, put others first, and maintain a peaceful environment. The playground peacemaker eventually becomes the office diplomat.

Being nice, polite, and selfless can lead to being underestimated and ostracized from a group. This seems unfair, but it is also likely true based on your experiences.

A deeper motivation likely drives the desire to be nice and accommodating. Other individuals do not always perceive these characteristics as positive or pleasant to be around. Avoiding assertiveness might lead to a negative impression of being selfless and generous. It's important to set boundaries and prioritize your own needs.

Reasons to Say No to Your Boss

Saying "no" to your boss can be challenging but sometimes necessary for various reasons. Here are legitimate reasons to say no to your boss:

Overload of Responsibilities: If your workload is already at its limit or if you're working on critical tasks, taking on additional responsibilities might compromise the quality of your work or lead to burnout. In such cases, it's essential to communicate with your boss about your current workload and explain why taking on more tasks at this moment could be detrimental to both your productivity and the quality of your work.

Conflicting Priorities: Sometimes, your boss may ask you to work on something that conflicts with your existing priorities or projects. In such situations, it's crucial to diplomatically express how the new task might impact your ability to meet existing deadlines or goals. You can propose alternative solutions or suggest reprioritizing tasks to accommodate the new request without sacrificing the quality of your work.

Lack of Expertise or Resources: If the task your boss assigns requires skills or resources you don't possess or have access to, it's reasonable to decline. Instead of accepting and potentially delivering subpar results, being upfront about your limitations is better. You can use this opportunity to discuss potential solutions, such as seeking additional training or resources, delegating the task to someone better suited, or exploring alternative approaches.

Ethical Concerns: If the task or request from your boss goes against your personal or professional ethics, it's crucial to stand firm and respectfully decline. Whether it involves unethical practices, conflicts of interest, or actions that could harm others, it's essential to prioritize integrity and moral values. When declining based on ethical concerns, explain why you cannot comply and, if possible, suggest alternative courses of action that align with ethical standards.

Health and Well-being: Your physical or mental health should never be compromised for work demands. Suppose your boss asks you to do something that could jeopardize your well-being, such as working excessive hours, skipping breaks, or engaging in tasks that exacerbate stress or anxiety. In that case, it's important to assert boundaries and prioritize self-care. Politely explain to your boss the impact the request could have on your health and productivity, and propose alternative solutions that promote a healthier work-life balance.

Legal Compliance: If the task or request from your boss violates company policies, industry regulations, or legal requirements, it's imperative to refuse. Compliance with laws and regulations is non-negotiable, and failure to adhere to them could have serious consequences for both you and the organization. Politely inform your boss of the legal implications and suggest ways to achieve the desired outcome within the boundaries of the law and company policies.

Personal Boundaries: There may be times when your boss's requests encroach upon your personal boundaries. This could involve working excessive hours, being constantly on call, or being asked to perform tasks beyond your job description's scope. It's essential to assert your boundaries respectfully but firmly, explaining why you're unable or unwilling to comply with certain requests. Emphasize the importance of work-life balance and maintaining your well-being to ensure long-term productivity and job satisfaction.

Strategic Misalignment: Raising your concerns is important if the task or project your boss is assigning does not align with the company's overall goals or strategic direction. Perhaps the proposed initiative conflicts with current market trends, lacks sufficient resources for successful implementation or diverts attention from more pressing priorities. Express your reservations constructively, providing evidence and insights to support your viewpoint. Engage in a dialogue with your boss to ensure alignment between individual tasks and broader organizational objectives.

Message Templates for Different Scenarios

Let's see some comprehensive toolkit of message templates designed to assist you in navigating various challenging scenarios with your boss. Each template is carefully crafted to help you communicate assertively, professionally, and effectively while still maintaining respect for your boss's position and fostering a constructive dialogue. Here are some scenarios covered and the corresponding message templates:

Saying No to Additional Work Assignments

Scenario Overview

Your boss approaches you with a new project or task that falls outside of your usual responsibilities. Perhaps you're already stretched thin with existing projects, or the new assignment doesn't align with your expertise or career goals. In such situations, it's crucial to communicate assertively and professionally while declining the additional workload.

V1. Declining a Project Outside Your Expertise (#001)

Re: New Project Opportunity

Dear [Boss's Name],

Thank you for considering me for the new project opportunity. While I appreciate your trust in my abilities, after carefully reviewing the project requirements, I believe it falls outside of my expertise in [specific area]. To ensure the project's success and uphold our quality standards, I recommend assigning this project to [colleague's name], who has extensive experience in this domain.

I remain committed to supporting the team's goals and am eager to contribute to projects where I can deliver the most value. Please let me know if there are any other ways I can assist in achieving our objectives.

Thank you for your understanding.

Best regards,

[Your Name]

V2. Managing Workload and Prioritizing Tasks (#002)

Re: Additional Task Request

Dear [Boss's Name],

I appreciate the opportunity to take on additional tasks and contribute to the team's efforts. However, after reviewing my current workload, I'm concerned about my ability to dedicate time and attention to new assignments without compromising the quality of existing projects.

I propose discussing priorities and potentially reallocating resources or adjusting deadlines to ensure that all projects receive the required focus. By strategically managing our workload, we can maintain our high standards and achieve our goals effectively.

Thank you for considering my perspective, and I look forward to collaborating to find the best way forward.

Warm regards,

[Your Name]

V3. Negotiating Timeframes for New Assignments (#003)

Re: New Assignment Deadline

Dear [Boss's Name],

Thank you for entrusting me with the new assignment. While I'm eager to contribute, I have concerns about the feasibility of the proposed deadline, given my current workload and other commitments.

To ensure that I can dedicate the necessary time and attention to this project and deliver quality results, I propose discussing alternative timelines that align with our capacity and resources. By setting realistic expectations, we can avoid unnecessary stress and ensure successful project outcomes.

I'm open to exploring solutions that meet our objectives while balancing work and personal responsibilities. Your guidance in finding a suitable timeframe would be greatly appreciated.

Thank you for your understanding and support.

Best regards,

[Your Name]

V4. Clarifying Your Availability for New Tasks (#004)

Re: New Task Assignment

Dear [Boss's Name],

Thank you for considering me for the new task assignment. While I'm committed to supporting the team's objectives, I want to ensure clarity regarding my current availability and workload.

At present, I am fully dedicated to [specific projects or tasks] and anticipate requiring focused attention to meet their deadlines and quality standards. Given this, I may not be able to take on additional responsibilities without compromising existing commitments.

I appreciate your understanding and am open to discussing potential solutions or alternative contributing ways that align with my current workload and priorities.

Thank you for your consideration.

Warm regards,

[Your Name]

V5. Expressing Gratitude and Declining Politely (#005)

Subject: Re: New Project Opportunity

Dear [Boss's Name],

I am grateful that you are considering me for the new project opportunity. While I'm honored by the offer, after careful consideration, I believe that my current workload does not allow me to take on additional responsibilities at this time.

I value your trust in my abilities and assure you that I remain fully committed to supporting the team's goals. If circumstances change in the future or if there are other ways I can contribute, please don't hesitate to let me know.

Thank you for your understanding and support.

Best regards,

[Your Name]

Pushing Back on Unreasonable Deadlines

Scenario Overview

Your boss assigns you a project with a tight deadline that you believe is unrealistic, given the scope of work and existing commitments. Pushing back on this deadline requires tact and diplomacy to communicate your concerns while still demonstrating your commitment to delivering quality work.

V1. Requesting Realistic Timeframes (#006)

Re: Project Deadline Discussion

Dear [Boss's Name],

I hope this message finds you well. I wanted to reach out regarding the deadline for the [project name] we discussed earlier. After reviewing the project requirements and considering my current workload, I have some concerns about the feasibility of the proposed deadline.

Given the complexity of the project and the need for thorough planning and execution, I believe that a more realistic timeframe would allow us to deliver the quality results we aim for. I propose discussing alternative timelines that take into account the intricacies of the project and allow for adequate time for review and revisions.

I'm fully committed to the success of this project and am confident that we can achieve our goals effectively with a realistic deadline. I'm open to your thoughts and suggestions on how best to proceed.

Thank you for your understanding and consideration.

Best regards,

[Your Name]

V2. Suggesting Alternative Approaches to Meet Deadlines (#007)

Re: Project Deadline Adjustment

Dear [Boss's Name],

I appreciate the opportunity to work on the [project name] and am excited about its possibilities. However, upon reviewing the project timeline, I have some reservations about the current deadline.

To ensure that we can meet our objectives without compromising on quality, I propose exploring alternative approaches that may help us streamline our processes and expedite certain tasks. This could include prioritizing key deliverables, reallocating resources, or seeking additional support where needed.

I believe we can still achieve our goals within a more realistic timeframe by adopting a more flexible and agile approach. I'm committed to working closely with you to implement these changes and ensure the success of the project.

Thank you for considering my input.

Warm regards,

[Your Name]

V3. Highlighting Potential Risks of Rushing (#008)

Concerns Regarding Project Deadline

Dear [Boss's Name],

I hope you're doing well. I wanted to share some concerns I have regarding the deadline for the [project name]. While I understand the urgency of the project, I'm worried that rushing through the process may compromise the quality of our work and increase the risk of errors.

Given the complexity of the project and the number of stakeholders involved, I believe it's crucial that we allow sufficient time for thorough planning, execution, and review. Rushing to meet an unrealistic deadline could lead to setbacks down the line and ultimately impact the project's success.

I propose reassessing the timeline and considering a more balanced approach that takes into account the need for quality and accuracy. By doing so, we can ensure that we deliver the best possible outcome for our team and stakeholders.

Thank you for your attention to this matter.

Best regards,

[Your Name]

V4. Presenting Data to Support Request (#009)

Proposal for Adjusting Project Deadline

Dear [Boss's Name],

I hope this email finds you well. I wanted to discuss the deadline for the [project name] and propose some adjustments based on my analysis of the project requirements and timelines.

After conducting a thorough review, it's become apparent that the current deadline may not allow us to fully meet the project's objectives while maintaining the desired level of quality. I've attached a brief analysis outlining the key milestones and potential risks associated with rushing through the project.

I believe that by extending the deadline by [proposed timeframe], we can mitigate these risks and ensure that we deliver a product that meets both our internal standards and the expectations of our stakeholders. I'm happy to discuss this further and provide any additional information needed to support this proposal.

Thank you for your consideration.

Best regards,

[Your Name]

V5. *Seeking Clarification on Priorities* (#010)

Clarification Regarding Project Deadline

Dear [Boss's Name],

I hope you're doing well. I wanted to touch base regarding the deadline for the [project name] to ensure we're aligned on expectations and priorities.

Given the current workload and the project's complexity, I want to confirm whether the proposed deadline is firm or if there's flexibility to adjust based on our progress and resource availability. This clarity will help us better plan and allocate our resources to ensure the project's success.

If there's room for discussion, I'm happy to explore alternative timelines or approaches that may better suit our needs and constraints. Your guidance on this matter would be greatly appreciated.

Thank you for your attention to this matter.

Best regards,

[Your Name]

Declining Meetings or Requests for Your Time

Scenario Overview

In today's fast-paced work environment, meetings and requests for your time can sometimes become overwhelming, making it challenging to balance competing priorities and manage your workload effectively. Politely declining meetings or requests for your time requires finesse and tact to communicate your availability while still demonstrating your commitment to collaboration and teamwork.

V1. Prioritizing Your Schedule (#011)

Unable to Attend [Meeting/Event]

Dear [Boss's Name],

I hope this email finds you well. Thank you for the invitation to [meeting/event]. Unfortunately, due to prior commitments and a full schedule, I regret to inform you that I won't be able to attend.

I understand the importance of the [meeting/event] and its relevance to our objectives. I've had to prioritize my time accordingly to ensure I can fulfill my current responsibilities effectively.

If there are specific agenda items or updates that require my input, please feel free to share them with me afterward, and I'll review them promptly.

Thank you for your understanding.

Best regards,

[Your Name]

V2. Offering Alternative Ways to Contribute (#012)

Alternative Input for [Meeting/Event]

Dear [Boss's Name],

I appreciate the opportunity to participate in the upcoming [meeting/event]. Unfortunately, due to conflicting commitments, I won't be able to attend in person.

However, I would still like to contribute to the discussions and provide input on the agenda topics. I can prepare a summary of my thoughts or suggestions beforehand and share them with you or the team for consideration during the meeting.

Please let me know if this approach works for you and if there are specific areas you'd like me to focus on.

Thank you for your understanding and flexibility.

Warm regards,

[Your Name]

V3. Proposing an Alternative Meeting Time (#013)

Request to Reschedule [Meeting/Event]

Dear [Boss's Name],

I hope this message finds you well. Thank you for scheduling the [meeting/event]. Unfortunately, due to a scheduling conflict, I won't be able to attend at the proposed time.

Could we reschedule the meeting for [alternative date/time]? This would allow me to fully participate and contribute to the discussion without any conflicts.

Please let me know if this alternative works for you, and I apologize for any inconvenience caused by the scheduling conflict.

Thank you for your understanding.

Best regards,

[Your Name]

V4. Delegating Attendance to a Colleague (#014)

Delegating Attendance for [Meeting/Event]

Dear [Boss's Name],

I hope this email finds you well. Thank you for the invitation to [meeting/event]. Unfortunately, due to a prior commitment, I won't be able to attend.

However, I've briefed [colleague's name] on the agenda topics and objectives of the meeting, and they are fully prepared to represent our team and provide any necessary input or updates. I'm confident that they will contribute effectively to the discussions.

Please let me know if there's anything specific you'd like me to convey to [colleague's name] before the meeting.

Thank you for your understanding and support.

Best regards,

[Your Name]

V5. *Expressing Gratitude and Declining Politely* (#015)

Regrets for [Meeting/Event]

Dear [Boss's Name],

I hope you're doing well. Thank you for inviting me to [meeting/event]. I appreciate the opportunity and the trust you've placed in me.

Unfortunately, I must decline the invitation due to a scheduling conflict. I regret any inconvenience this may cause and hope the meeting goes smoothly.

Please keep me updated on any key outcomes or decisions made during the meeting, and I'll catch up afterward.

Thank you for your understanding.

Warm regards,

[Your Name]

Saying No to Unreasonable Requests for Overtime or Off-Hours Work:

Scenario Overview

In a competitive and demanding work environment, it's not uncommon for employees to face requests to work overtime or during off-hours. While occasional flexibility may be necessary, consistently being asked to work beyond regular hours can lead to burnout, decreased morale, and diminished productivity. Politely declining unreasonable requests for overtime or off-hours work is essential for maintaining a healthy work-life balance and ensuring your well-being.

V1. Asserting Work-Life Balance (#016)

Re: Overtime Request

Dear [Boss's Name],

I hope this message finds you well. Thank you for considering me for the overtime request. However, I must respectfully decline the additional hours at this time.

Maintaining a healthy work-life balance is crucial for my well-being and productivity. While I'm committed to meeting deadlines and contributing to the team's success, I believe it's essential to prioritize self-care and avoid burnout.

I'm confident that, with effective time management and resource allocation during regular working hours, we can still achieve our goals without needing overtime. Please feel free to discuss any alternative solutions or adjustments to the workload.

Thank you for your understanding and support.

Best regards,

[Your Name]

V2. Negotiating Compromise or Compensation (#017)

Re: Off-Hours Work Request

Dear [Boss's Name],

I appreciate the opportunity to assist with the request for work off-hours. However, I must express my concerns about the impact on my work-life balance.

Given the situation's urgency, I'm open to exploring alternative solutions or compromises. These could include adjusting deadlines, reallocating resources, or compensating for the additional time worked.

I remain dedicated to meeting our objectives and delivering quality work. Please let me know if there's room for negotiation or if there are alternative approaches we can consider.

Thank you for your understanding and cooperation.

Warm regards,

[Your Name]

V3. Expressing Prior Commitments (#018)

Re: Request for Overtime

Dear [Boss's Name],

I hope you're doing well. I appreciate the opportunity to contribute to [project/task]. However, I regret to inform you that I cannot accommodate the request for overtime due to prior commitments.

I'm fully committed to meeting our deadlines and ensuring the project's success within regular working hours. If there are ways to streamline processes or adjust priorities to accommodate the workload, I'm more than willing to discuss them.

Thank you for your understanding.

Best regards,

[Your Name]

V4. Suggesting Alternative Solutions (#019)

Re: Off-Hours Work Request

Dear [Boss's Name],

Thank you for considering me for the off-hours work request. However, I believe there may be alternative solutions that could address the situation's urgency without requiring additional hours.

For example, we could explore delegating specific tasks to other team members or adjusting project timelines to accommodate the workload more effectively. I'm confident that with careful planning and collaboration, we can find a solution that meets our objectives without sacrificing work-life balance.

Please let me know if you'd like to discuss these alternatives further.

Thank you for your understanding and consideration.

Warm regards,

[Your Name]

V5. Reaffirming Commitment to Quality and Efficiency (#020)

Subject: Re: Overtime Request

Dear [Boss's Name],

I appreciate the opportunity to assist with the overtime request. However, I must prioritize maintaining a healthy work-life balance to ensure my continued effectiveness and productivity.

I'm committed to delivering quality work within regular working hours and believe effective time management and collaboration can help us achieve our goals without needing overtime.

Thank you for your understanding and support.

Best regards,

[Your Name]

Rejecting Unreasonable Expectations or Demands

Scenario Overview

In the workplace, it's not uncommon to encounter situations where you're presented with unreasonable expectations or demands from your boss. These could include unrealistic deadlines, excessive workloads, or requests outside your job scope. Rejecting such expectations or demands requires careful communication to maintain professionalism and assert your boundaries effectively.x

V1. *Prioritizing Work-Life Balance* (#021)

Request for Overtime

Dear [Boss's Name],

I hope this message finds you well. Thank you for considering me for the overtime request. However, at this time, I must prioritize my work-life balance to maintain my well-being and effectiveness.

While I understand the importance of meeting deadlines and supporting the team, consistent overtime can lead to burnout and reduced productivity in the long run. I believe managing workload effectively during regular working hours is crucial to ensure sustainable performance.

I'm committed to delivering quality work within established timelines and am open to discussing alternative strategies for meeting project objectives without relying on overtime.

Thank you for your understanding.

Best regards,

[Your Name]

V2. *Clarifying Personal Commitments* (#022)

Off-Hours Work Request

Dear [Boss's Name],

I appreciate the opportunity to assist with the request for work off-hours. However, I have prior personal commitments during the requested time frame that I cannot reschedule.

While I'm dedicated to supporting the team and meeting project deadlines, I must honor my existing obligations outside of work. I believe that maintaining a healthy work-life balance is essential for sustained productivity and well-being.

If the deadline is flexible or if there are alternative ways I can contribute within regular working hours, please let me know, and I'll be happy to assist.

Thank you for your understanding.

Warm regards,

[Your Name]

V3. Proposing Alternative Solutions (#023)

Re: Urgent Project Assistance

Dear [Boss's Name],

Thank you for reaching out regarding the urgent project assistance. While I understand the importance of the deadline, I'm concerned about the impact of working overtime on my overall well-being and performance.

Instead of working overtime, I propose reallocating resources or adjusting project priorities to meet the deadline effectively. We can maintain quality standards by streamlining processes or redistributing tasks without requiring additional hours outside of regular work.

I'm committed to finding a solution that meets both the project's needs and my personal boundaries. Please let me know your thoughts on this approach.

Thank you for your consideration.

Best regards,

[Your Name]

V4. *Reinforcing Commitment to Quality* (#024)

Re: Weekend Work Request

Dear [Boss's Name],

I appreciate your understanding of the urgent nature of the project, which requires weekend work. While I'm committed to delivering quality results, I believe it's important to consider the potential impact of working outside of regular hours on productivity and well-being.

To ensure that we maintain the high standards we strive for, I suggest exploring alternative solutions or adjustments to the project timeline. By carefully managing our workload and prioritizing tasks, we can achieve our objectives within regular working hours without compromising quality.

Thank you for your understanding and cooperation.

Warm regards,

[Your Name]

V5. *Seeking Support for Boundaries* (#025)

Request for Additional Work Hours

Dear [Boss's Name],

I hope you're doing well. I wanted to address the request for additional work hours. While I understand the urgency of the situation, consistent overtime may not be sustainable in the long term.

I believe it's essential to maintain a healthy work-life balance to ensure sustained productivity and well-being. As such, I kindly request your support in managing workload expectations and finding alternative solutions that allow us to meet project deadlines without relying solely on overtime.

Thank you for your understanding and support in this matter.

Best regards,

[Your Name]

Case Studies

Let's look at case studies and real-life examples to illustrate the scenarios of declining unreasonable requests for overtime or off-hours work:

Case Study 1: Prioritizing Work-Life Balance

Scenario: Sarah, a marketing manager at a fast-paced advertising agency, consistently receives requests from her supervisor to work overtime to meet tight client deadlines. Concerned about the impact on her well-being and personal life, Sarah decides to decline the latest request for overtime work.

Response: Sarah schedules a meeting with her supervisor to discuss the request. She acknowledges the importance of meeting client deadlines but emphasizes the need to maintain a healthy work-life balance. Sarah proposes alternative strategies for managing the workload within regular hours, such as reallocating resources or adjusting project timelines. Her supervisor appreciates her proactive approach and agrees to explore alternative solutions while respecting Sarah's boundaries.

Case Study 2: Clarifying Personal Commitments

Scenario: Alex, a software developer, is asked to work on a critical project over the weekend. However, Alex has prior personal commitments that he cannot reschedule. Unsure of how to decline the request without appearing uncooperative, Alex decides to communicate his personal commitments to his manager.

Response: Alex sends an email to his manager, expressing gratitude for the opportunity to assist with the project. He explains his prior personal commitments over the weekend and highlights his dedication to meeting project deadlines. Alex suggests alternative solutions, such as delegating tasks to other team members or adjusting the project timeline, to ensure that the project stays on track without requiring him to work overtime. His manager appreciates his transparency and collaborates with him to find a suitable solution that accommodates Alex's personal commitments.

Case Study 3: Proposing Alternative Solutions

Scenario: James, a sales representative, is asked to attend a client meeting outside of regular business hours. Concerned about the impact on his work-life balance, James decides to propose alternative solutions to his supervisor.

Response: James schedules a meeting with his supervisor to discuss the client meeting request. He acknowledges the importance of the meeting but expresses his concerns about working outside of regular hours. James proposes alternative solutions, such as rescheduling the meeting during regular business hours or arranging a virtual meeting to accommodate everyone's schedules. His supervisor appreciates his proactive approach and agrees to explore alternative options that meet both the client's needs and James's work-life balance requirements.

HOW TO SAY NO TO EMPLOYEES

Handling employee requests can be overwhelming, especially when they need to be declined. However, it's crucial to remember that a denied request doesn't have to lead to negative emotions or a sense of hopelessness. By employing the right strategies, these situations can actually be turned into opportunities to foster workplace learning, transparency, and empathy. This guide is designed to equip you with these tactics, helping you navigate denied employee requests in a way that maintains morale and promotes a positive workplace culture.

Today's workforce is more vocal about their needs and preferences, which generally benefits employees and organizations. Open communication about employee expectations strengthens company culture and encourages firms to prioritize employee satisfaction, which can have significant long-term benefits. However, managing high expectations and the subsequent increase in employee requests, some of which may not be feasible, can be a challenge. While it's acceptable to decline a request, it's crucial to do so in a manner that doesn't undermine morale, emphasizing the importance of effective communication in such situations.

Although the Great Resignation has been declared over, it has made us realize that today's employees are less inclined to tolerate a company that fails to meet their expectations. This is especially true for Millennials and Generation Z personnel. Younger workers tend to stay in jobs for shorter periods than Baby Boomers or Gen Xers, and they are more likely to pursue new opportunities, so it is critical to meet their requirements before seeking elsewhere.

What do employee demands look like now? A Gartner study identified aspects that employees deem "very important" in their jobs. Pay (64% rated it as "very important"), work-life balance and well-being (61%), the ability to use their best skills (58%), and attention to DE&I (42%). It is unsurprising that these elements appear frequently in employee demands.

Employees may leave if they believe they are not being heard and appreciated. Thus, taking employee requests seriously and providing reasonable concessions is critical. However, it is impossible to always provide every employee with the information they seek. You may not have the financial or other resources to comply. Perhaps the request does not correspond with the company's principles, or you do not want to set a precedent by creating an exception to organizational policy.

Having to say no to a request can be challenging. You'll need to handle it cautiously to avoid dissatisfaction and, in some situations, prevent staff from leaving for other firms. If you do it correctly, your employees will understand that there are no hard feelings and may even leave feeling empowered.

Tips for How to Say No to Employee Requests

Set Yourself Up for Success

When it comes to saying no to an employee request, having a solid basis in the form of policy is beneficial. Employees will be more understanding if you can back up your comments with an official business, department, or team position on the subject. You might even be able to prevent a request from being made in the first place if staff can look up the regulations before submitting their inquiries. There will always be people who make requests that they know violate policies, but at least they'll be prepared for your response and the logic behind it.

Employees will be more understanding if you can back up your comments with an official business, department, or team position on the subject.

Utilize your digital technology to spread the news about corporate policies such as pay evaluations, benefits, and PTO restrictions. Hosting this material on a searchable platform like your intranet ensures that employees can access all necessary information.

Acknowledge and Clarify

Employees need to feel heard, which is linked to increased engagement and a sense of efficacy at work. Employees who make unsuccessful requests mustn't feel ignored or dismissed.

A seemingly impulsive refusal can elicit feelings of disrespect. Even if you have a compelling reason to say no, you must demonstrate that you have considered what the employee has to say. That entails listening, asking questions to gather any necessary information, and clarifying what is being asked. After the conversation, you can gently explain why you are unable to accept the employee's request (more on this later). Though the employee may be upset with the outcome, they will feel less hurt if they know you have carefully examined their concerns.

Provide a Legitimate Reason

Remember how annoying it was when your parents answered your "why?" with the dreaded words, "Because I said so?" Failure to provide an explanation makes the requestee feel helpless. If you can explain the (valid) rationale for your refusal, you will receive less pushback and less dissatisfaction from the employee.

Make it clear why you're declining the employee's request. Is it a budgetary issue? Does the request violate a specific company policy? Has a similar idea been attempted before with negative results? Share this with the employees, and they will be more likely to view things your way.

Offer a Plan B

If something special about an employee's request makes it unworkable, try to work with them on an alternative. For example, suggest a better time if the timing doesn't work for an extended vacation request. Alternatively, let them spend the time away but organize a few remote work days throughout their trip so that they can check in with the team.

If something special about an employee's request makes it unworkable, try to work with them on an alternative. Opening the conversation and demonstrating your willingness to compromise informs employees that you genuinely want to meet their requirements, even if it is not exactly how they envisioned it.

Do Not Leave Employees Hanging

Nobody loves to be the bad guy. It is extremely difficult to say no when you care about your staff and want them to be as happy at work as possible. However, there are occasions when you are unable to say yes.

The worst thing you can do is offer staff false optimism by extending the time it takes to say no. Communicate your refusal as early as possible so the employee can come to terms with your answer, and you can both go on. They will appreciate you being open, and you'll fret less about delivering the terrible news.

Express Empathy Without Faltering

Whatever decision you make, remember the human side of an employee request. Consider the employee's point of view. Human-centered leadership is a prominent workplace trend for 2024, with 82% of employees believing their firm must perceive them as individuals rather than just employees. This makes it more crucial than ever to empathize with employees' requests and demonstrate that you understand their perspective.

For example, if an employee requests new technology that you do not currently have the funds for, it is OK to acknowledge their unhappiness. Communicate that you understand why they are asking and that you are sorry to inform them that it is not possible now. After that, don't forget about the need they've voiced; it may be able to meet it differently or revisit the request later.

82% of employees believe their employer must view them "as a person, not just an employee." Empathize with them.

Recognizing an employee's displeasure or other difficult feelings while maintaining your ground is a fine line to tread. You'll want to demonstrate your concern without creating any opportunity for pushback or false hope. This can be tough to perfect at first, but with experience, you'll learn to be understanding while remaining firm.

Offer Feedback and Express Gratitude

Employee requests are frequently personal and relate to accomplishments, projects, or causes that the individual is particularly passionate about. This might create a difficult scenario when you have to say no, but simple praise and recognition can help cushion the impact.

Perhaps one employee is pleased with how a project has progressed and wants to take it to the next level, but the team has too many other priorities to make it happen. Or perhaps they've put in extra work and produced excellent results this quarter, but you won't be able to raise them due to budget constraints. In certain instances, a denial may appear to be a rejection—the employee may believe that all of their efforts have gone unnoticed.

To avoid this, acknowledge their hard work. Provide positive comments while you explain why you are declining the request, then follow up with further praise in the days and weeks following the chat. Employee appreciation will help decouple the individual's self-worth from the fact that their request was denied and prevent a drop in motivation in the future.

Keep the Big Picture in Mind

If the employee in question is upset, dissatisfied, or angry about your choice, address these sentiments honestly and try to provide an open platform for conversation. When resentment simmers, it can create disengagement and have a detrimental impact on your corporate culture.

Some demands, even if they must be denied, indicate bigger issues with an employee's function, overall job satisfaction, or organizational policies. Paying attention and utilizing this as an employee listening opportunity is your responsibility. Determine the source of your employee's dissatisfaction and assess whether others share this sentiment. It's possible (and even likely) that this person is not alone in their displeasure.

Some requests, even if they must be denied, indicate a deeper issue. It's your responsibility to pay attention.

Is the request a wake-up call for a policy that needs to be revised or a cultural norm that requires clarification? Although you may need to say no right now, it may draw your attention to a weakness that needs action. Looking at denied requests from a broader perspective allows you to use them to improve the situation for all employees.

Message Templates for Different Scenarios

This section provides a comprehensive collection of message templates designed to help you effectively communicate boundaries and navigate difficult conversations with employees, even your boss. Each template is tailored to address common scenarios encountered in the workplace, providing a structured framework for asserting yourself while maintaining professionalism and respect. Let's see some message templates included:

Saying No to Requests for Unreasonable Deadlines

Before crafting a response to a request for an unreasonable deadline, it's essential to understand the context surrounding the request. Consider factors such as the urgency of the task, the feasibility of meeting the deadline given available resources, and the potential impact on other projects or responsibilities. Understanding the context allows you to tailor your response accordingly and effectively communicate your rationale.

V1. Firm but Considerate Response (#026)

Re: Deadline Extension Request

Hi [Employee's Name],

Thank you for bringing up the deadline extension request for [project/task]. I understand the importance of meeting deadlines, and I appreciate your diligence in ensuring the project's success.

After thorough consideration and assessment of our current workload and resources, it's clear that accommodating the requested extension would compromise the quality of our work and potentially impact other projects' timelines. Therefore, we must maintain the original deadline.

I'm committed to supporting you in any way possible to ensure we meet our goals effectively. Let's brainstorm alternative strategies or resource allocations to facilitate a smooth project completion.

Your understanding and cooperation are greatly appreciated.

Best regards,

[Your Name]

V2. Suggesting a Realistic Alternative (#027)

Re: Urgent Project Deadline

Hi [Employee's Name],

Thank you for reaching out regarding the urgent project deadline. I understand the time-sensitive nature of the task and our desire to deliver exceptional results.

However, upon reviewing our current workload and team capacity, it's evident that meeting the requested deadline would require unrealistic effort and could compromise the quality of our deliverables.

To ensure we maintain quality standards and effectively manage our resources, I suggest extending the deadline by [specific timeframe]. This would allow us to allocate the necessary time and resources to complete the project successfully without sacrificing quality.

I'm open to discussing this further and exploring any concerns or alternative solutions you may have.

Thank you for your understanding and collaboration.

Regards,

[Your Name]

V3. Assertive Refusal with Reasoning (#028)

Re: Deadline Extension Request for [Project Name]

Hi [Employee's Name],

I appreciate your promptness in addressing the deadline extension request for [project]. I understand the urgency and importance of completing the task on time.

After carefully considering and evaluating our current workload and project priorities, I regret to inform you that we cannot extend the deadline for [project]. The requested extension would create conflicts with other projects and impact our overall project timeline.

I value your dedication and commitment to your work. Let's discuss how we can adjust our approach or resource allocation to ensure we meet our deadlines effectively while maintaining quality standards.

Thank you for your understanding and cooperation.

Best regards,

[Your Name]

V4. Offering Support and Collaboration (#029)

Re: Urgent Deadline Request

Hi [Employee's Name],

Thank you for bringing up the urgent deadline request for [task/project]. I understand the importance of meeting our commitments and delivering results promptly.

However, after reviewing our current workload and team capacity, it's clear that meeting the requested deadline would stretch our resources thin and compromise the quality of our deliverables.

I'm committed to supporting you in finding alternative solutions to meet our goals effectively. Let's brainstorm together and explore ways to streamline our processes or reallocate resources to ensure successful project completion within a realistic timeframe.

Your flexibility and collaboration are greatly appreciated.

Regards,

[Your Name]

V5. Clarifying Expectations and Offering Alternatives (#030)

Re: Deadline Extension Request for [Project Name]

Hi [Employee's Name],

Thank you for bringing up the deadline extension request for [project]. I understand the importance of delivering quality work within a reasonable timeframe.

However, given our current workload and project priorities, extending the deadline for [project] would impact other projects' timelines and deliverables.

I suggest revisiting the project timeline and adjusting our approach or resource allocation accordingly to ensure we meet our commitments effectively. Let's discuss optimizing our processes and prioritizing tasks to meet our goals without compromising quality.

I appreciate your understanding and collaboration in this matter.

Best regards,

[Your Name]

Declining Requests for Time Off

When declining requests for time off, handling the situation delicately is essential while maintaining professionalism and respect for the employee's needs. It's crucial to be respectful and transparent and provide reasons when appropriate.

V1. Standard Request Denial (#031)

Dear [Employee's Name],

Thank you for submitting your request for time off. After carefully considering our current workload and staffing needs, we regret to inform you that we cannot approve your request for [dates requested]. We understand the importance of your time off, and we encourage you to resubmit your request at a later date when our operational demands allow for it.

Thank you for your understanding.

Sincerely,

[Your Name]

[Your Position]

***V2**. Urgent Work Prioritization (#032)*

Dear [Employee's Name],

I appreciate your recent request for time off. Unfortunately, due to the unexpected urgency of [specific project/task], we are unable to accommodate your request for time off during the requested dates. Your contribution to this project is crucial at this time, and we need your expertise to ensure its successful completion.

I understand this may be disappointing news, and I assure you that your time off will be considered a priority once this urgent matter is resolved.

Thank you for your flexibility and understanding.

Regards,

[Your Name]

[Your Position]

***V3**. Holiday/Peak Period Limitations (#033)*

Dear [Employee's Name],

Thank you for submitting your request for time off during the upcoming holiday/peak period. Unfortunately, due to high demand and staffing constraints during this time, we are unable to grant additional time off requests beyond what has already been approved.

We encourage you to plan your time off in advance for future holidays or consider alternative dates that may better accommodate our operational needs.

Thank you for your cooperation and understanding.

Best regards,

[Your Name]

[Your Position]

V4. Conflict with Existing Requests (#034)

Dear [Employee's Name],

I hope this message finds you well. I wanted to inform you that we have received multiple time off requests for the same dates, and unfortunately, we are unable to approve all requests due to staffing limitations.

After careful consideration, we regret to inform you that your request for time off during [dates requested] conflicts with existing approved requests. We understand the importance of your planned time off and encourage you to consider alternative dates.

Thank you for your understanding and cooperation in this matter.

Warm regards,

[Your Name]

[Your Position]

V5. Policy Adherence (#035)

Dear [Employee's Name],

Thank you for your recent request for time off. While we appreciate your commitment to your personal well-being, I regret to inform you that your request does not comply with our company's time off policy, which requires [specify policy violation, e.g., a minimum notice period, limit on concurrent leave, etc.].

I encourage you to review the company's policy and resubmit your request in accordance with the guidelines provided.

Thank you for your attention to this matter.

Best regards,

[Your Name]

[Your Position]

Rejecting Project Proposals or Ideas

Rejecting project proposals or ideas can be delicate, as it involves providing constructive feedback while maintaining a positive relationship with the employee or team member. Here are some message templates tailored for rejecting project proposals or ideas:

V1. Appreciative Feedback with Explanation (#036)

Dear [Employee's Name],

Thank you for submitting your project proposal. I appreciate the effort and creativity you've put into it. However, after careful review and consideration, we have decided not to move forward with this idea.

While the proposal aligns with our goals in some aspects, we believe there are opportunities for improvement in [specific areas, e.g., feasibility, alignment with company strategy, market demand]. I encourage you to revisit the proposal, address these areas, and resubmit it for further consideration.

Thank you for your dedication and contribution to our team's initiatives.

Best regards,

[Your Name]

[Your Position]

V2. Positive Reinforcement with Suggestion for Alternative Approach (#037)

Dear [Employee's Name],

I want to express my appreciation for your recent project proposal. Your enthusiasm and creativity are truly valued within our team.

After a thorough evaluation, we have decided not to proceed with this particular idea. However, I believe there is potential for further exploration by focusing on [specific aspect or angle] to better align with our current objectives. I encourage you to consider revising the proposal with this in mind.

Thank you for your continuous efforts and dedication to driving innovation within our team.

Warm regards,

[Your Name]

[Your Position]

V3. Constructive Feedback with Explanation of Decision (#038)

Dear [Employee's Name],

Thank you for submitting your project proposal. I've carefully reviewed the details you provided. While I appreciate your creativity and effort, we have decided not to pursue this idea at this time.

The decision is based on [specific reasons, e.g., market research findings, resource constraints, strategic priorities]. I encourage you to continue exploring new ideas and initiatives, as your innovative thinking is instrumental to our team's success.

Thank you for your understanding and contributions.

Sincerely,

[Your Name]

[Your Position]

V4. Encouragement for Future Submissions (#039)

Dear [Employee's Name],

Thank you for sharing your project proposal with us. Your commitment to driving new initiatives is commendable and greatly appreciated.

After careful consideration, we have determined that this particular idea is not the best fit for our current objectives. Nevertheless, I encourage you to continue generating ideas and submitting proposals. Your creativity and initiative are valuable assets to our team, and I'm confident that your next idea will contribute significantly to our success.

Thank you for your ongoing dedication.

Best regards,

[Your Name]

[Your Position]

V5. Invitation for Discussion and Collaboration (#040)

Dear [Employee's Name],

Thank you for presenting your project proposal. I appreciate the effort you've invested in developing this idea.

After a thorough evaluation, we have decided not to proceed with this proposal. However, I believe there is potential for collaboration and refinement to align it with our objectives better. I encourage you to schedule a meeting to discuss potential adjustments and explore how we can work together to enhance the proposal.

Your willingness to innovate and collaborate is invaluable to our team's success, and I look forward to our discussion.

Warm regards,

[Your Name]

[Your Position]

Refusing Unreasonable Demands or Expectations

Refusing unreasonable demands or expectations while maintaining professionalism and respect for the employee's perspective is crucial for effective communication. Here are some message templates tailored for refusing unreasonable demands or expectations:

V1. Firm yet Respectful Response (#041)

Dear [Employee's Name],

I appreciate your dedication and commitment to your work. However, after careful consideration of the recent demand/expectation you've raised, I regret to inform you that it is not feasible within our current resources and priorities.

I understand your perspective and am open to discussing alternative solutions that align better with our capabilities and objectives. Let's schedule a meeting to explore other options together.

Thank you for your understanding and cooperation.

Best regards,

[Your Name]

[Your Position]

V2. Setting Boundaries and Explaining Constraints (#042)

Dear [Employee's Name],

Thank you for bringing your expectations to my attention. While I value your input and dedication, it's important to recognize the limitations within which we must operate.

Unfortunately, the demand/expectation you've expressed exceeds our current resources and may not align with our strategic priorities. I'm more than willing to discuss this further and explore alternative more feasible approaches.

Thank you for your understanding.

Warm regards,

[Your Name]

[Your Position]

V3. Clarifying Priorities and Redirecting Focus (#043)

Dear [Employee's Name],

I want to acknowledge your request and your commitment to achieving success in your role. However, upon reviewing the demand/expectation you've presented, I believe it may not be in line with our current priorities.

Our focus at the moment is on [specific priorities or projects], and allocating resources to address your request may divert attention from these critical initiatives. I'm open to discussing this further and finding a solution aligning with our goals.

Thank you for your understanding and cooperation.

Sincerely,

[Your Name]

[Your Position]

V4. Emphasizing Realistic Expectations (#044)

Dear [Employee's Name],

I appreciate your enthusiasm and dedication to your work. However, the demand/expectation you've articulated appears to be beyond what we can reasonably accommodate at this time.

It's important for us to set realistic expectations and allocate resources effectively to ensure the success of our projects. I'm open to discussing this further and finding a solution that works for both parties.

Thank you for your understanding and flexibility.

Best regards,

[Your Name]

[Your Position]

V5. Reiterating Organizational Constraints (#045)

Dear [Employee's Name],

Thank you for bringing your concerns to my attention. While I understand the importance of your request, it's essential to consider the broader organizational constraints and priorities.

Given our current resources and commitments, fulfilling the demand/ expectation you've outlined may not be feasible without compromising other essential aspects of our operations. I'm willing to discuss this further and explore alternative approaches that align better with our capabilities.

Thank you for your understanding and collaboration.

Warm regards,

[Your Name]

[Your Position]

Setting Limits on Workload or Scope

Setting limits on workload or scope is crucial for maintaining productivity, managing resources effectively, and preventing burnout among employees. Here are some message templates that exposit how to communicate these boundaries professionally and respectfully.

V1. Clarification of Priorities and Capacity (#046)

Dear [Employee's Name],

I appreciate your dedication and enthusiasm for taking on additional responsibilities. However, after evaluating our current workload and resources, it's essential to ensure that we maintain a manageable scope to deliver high-quality results.

At this time, I must ask that we refrain from taking on any further projects beyond our agreed-upon priorities to prevent overload and maintain focus on our key objectives. I value your contributions and want to ensure that we can give each task the attention it deserves.

Thank you for your understanding and cooperation.

Best regards,

[Your Name]

[Your Position]

V2. Setting Clear Expectations and Boundaries (#047)

Dear [Employee's Name],

I want to express my gratitude for your hard work and dedication to your role.

As we continue to navigate our workload, it's essential to establish clear boundaries to ensure that we maintain a sustainable pace.

Moving forward, I kindly request that we refrain from taking on any additional projects beyond our current commitments. It's crucial to prioritize our tasks effectively and maintain a healthy balance to avoid overwhelm and maintain quality standards.

Thank you for your cooperation in adhering to these boundaries.

Warm regards,

[Your Name]

[Your Position]

V3. Reinforcement of Work-Life Balance (#048)

Dear [Employee's Name],

Your commitment to your work is commendable, and I appreciate your willingness to take on new challenges. However, it's crucial to prioritize our well-being and maintain a healthy work-life balance.

I want to ensure that we manage our workload effectively to prevent burnout and maintain productivity. Therefore, I kindly request that we refrain from expanding our scope beyond what is manageable within our current capacity.

Thank you for your understanding and cooperation in preserving our well-being.

Best regards,

[Your Name]

[Your Position]

V4. Acknowledgment of Current Commitments (#044)

Dear [Employee's Name],

I want to express my appreciation for your dedication and hard work on our ongoing projects. As we continue to move forward, it's important to acknowledge our current commitments and ensure that we can fulfill them effectively.

To maintain the quality of our work and avoid overextending ourselves, I kindly request that we refrain from taking on any additional tasks or projects at this time. Let's focus on completing our existing commitments before considering new opportunities.

Thank you for your understanding and collaboration.

Sincerely,

[Your Name]

[Your Position]

V5. Encouragement for Open Communication (#045)

Dear [Employee's Name],

Your contributions to our team have been invaluable, and I appreciate your dedication to excellence. As we manage our workload and priorities, it's essential to maintain open communication to ensure that we're aligned on our objectives and limitations.

If you feel that our workload is becoming overwhelming or that we're stretching ourselves too thin, I encourage you to speak up so that we can address any concerns and adjust accordingly. Let's work together to ensure that we maintain a sustainable pace and deliver our best work.

Thank you for your commitment to our team's success.

Warm regards,

[Your Name]

[Your Position]

Communicating Policy Enforcement or Rule Adherence

When establishing boundaries with employees, it's crucial to communicate well while maintaining professionalism and respect for their roles and contributions. Here are some message templates on how to effectively communicate boundaries:

V1. Setting Clear Expectations (#046)

Dear [Employee's Name],

I wanted to touch base regarding our upcoming projects and priorities. As we move forward, we must establish clear boundaries to ensure we can effectively manage our workload and deliver quality results.

Moving forward, I kindly request that we focus on the core responsibilities outlined in our job descriptions and agreed-upon project objectives. While it's natural to feel enthusiastic about exploring new opportunities, maintaining focus on our designated tasks will help us achieve our goals efficiently.

Thank you for your understanding and commitment to our team's success.

Warm regards,

[Your Name]

[Your Position]

V2. Clarifying Availability and Accessibility (#047)

Dear [Employee's Name],

I appreciate your dedication to your work and your willingness to go above and beyond to support our team's objectives. However, I've noticed that there have been instances where your availability outside of regular working hours has been consistently required.

While occasional flexibility is expected, it's important to establish boundaries to ensure a healthy work-life balance for both yourself and the team. Moving forward, I encourage you to prioritize your well-being and limit work-related communications outside of designated work hours unless it's an emergency.

Thank you for your understanding and cooperation in maintaining a healthy balance.

Best regards,

[Your Name]

[Your Position]

V3. Reinforcing Professional Conduct (#048)

Dear [Employee's Name],

I wanted to address a recent incident regarding [specific behavior or action] that occurred in the workplace. While I understand that situations can be challenging, it's essential for us to maintain a professional and respectful environment at all times.

Moving forward, I kindly request that we adhere to our company's code of conduct and treat each other with courtesy and respect. Open communication and constructive feedback are encouraged, but it's important to ensure that discussions remain professional and focused on finding solutions.

Thank you for your attention to this matter.

Sincerely,

[Your Name]

[Your Position]

V4. *Managing Workload and Priorities* (#049)

Dear [Employee's Name],

As we continue to navigate our workload and project commitments, I wanted to touch base regarding our capacity to take on additional tasks or projects. While showing initiative and enthusiasm is admirable, it's important to ensure we can effectively manage our workload without sacrificing quality or efficiency.

Moving forward, I kindly request that we prioritize our current tasks and commitments before considering new opportunities. This will help us maintain focus and deliver our best work while avoiding overload and burnout.

Thank you for your understanding and cooperation in managing our workload effectively.

Warm regards,

[Your Name]

[Your Position]

V5. Respecting Personal Boundaries (#050)

Dear [Employee's Name],

I wanted to discuss the importance of respecting personal boundaries in the workplace. While collaboration and teamwork are essential for our success, it's crucial to recognize and respect each other's individual space and preferences.

Moving forward, I kindly request that we refrain from intruding on personal space or engaging in conversations or actions that may make others feel uncomfortable. It's important to foster a supportive and inclusive environment where everyone feels respected and valued.

Thank you for your attention to this matter.

Best regards,

[Your Name]

[Your Position]

Handling Employee Disputes

Handling employee disputes or conflicts requires careful navigation to ensure a fair resolution while maintaining professionalism and respect for all parties involved. Here are some message templates on how to effectively address and resolve employee disputes or conflicts:

V1. *Acknowledgment of the Dispute* (#051)

Dear [Employee's Name],

I understand that there has been a disagreement between you and [other party/colleague] regarding [brief description of the issue]. It's important for us to address these concerns promptly to ensure a harmonious work environment for everyone.

I appreciate your willingness to communicate openly about this matter, and I want to assure you that we will work together to find a fair and satisfactory resolution for all parties involved.

Let's schedule a meeting to discuss the situation further and explore potential solutions.

Best regards,

[Your Name]

[Your Position]

V2. *Encouragement for Open Communication* (#052)

Dear [Employee's Name],

I've been informed of the recent disagreement between you and [other party/colleague] regarding [brief description of the issue]. Open communication is key to resolving conflicts effectively, and I appreciate your willingness to address this matter directly.

I encourage you to express your concerns and perspectives openly and constructively during our upcoming meeting. By listening to each other's viewpoints and working together, I'm confident that we can find a mutually agreeable solution.

Thank you for your cooperation in resolving this issue.

Warm regards,

[Your Name]

[Your Position]

V3. Facilitation of Mediation (#053)

Dear [Employee's Name],

I understand that there has been a disagreement between you and [other party/colleague] regarding [brief description of the issue]. To ensure a fair and impartial resolution, I would like to propose a mediation session where we can discuss the matter in a neutral and supportive environment.

During the mediation session, both parties can share their perspectives and concerns, and I will act as a mediator to facilitate constructive dialogue and find a mutually acceptable solution.

Please let me know your availability for the mediation session, and I will coordinate accordingly.

Best regards,

[Your Name]

[Your Position]

V4. Emphasis on Finding Common Ground (#054)

Dear [Employee's Name],

I've been made aware of the recent disagreement between you and [other party/colleague] regarding [brief description of the issue]. While conflicts are inevitable in any workplace, it's essential for us to approach this situation with a focus on finding common ground and reaching a mutually acceptable solution.

Our shared goal is to ensure a positive and productive work environment for everyone. Let's use our upcoming meeting to identify areas of agreement and explore potential compromises that address each other's concerns.

Thank you for your cooperation and commitment to resolving this issue amicably.

Warm regards,

[Your Name]

[Your Position]

V5. Reassurance of Support (#055)

Dear [Employee's Name],

I understand that you've disagreed with [other party/colleague] regarding [brief description of the issue]. I want to assure you that your concerns are important to me, and I'm committed to helping resolve this matter to your satisfaction.

We will carefully review the situation during our meeting and explore potential solutions together. Your perspective and input are valuable, and I encourage you to share any additional information or concerns you may have.

Thank you for your patience and cooperation as we work towards a resolution.

Best regards,

[Your Name]

[Your Position]

Case Studies

Real-life scenarios and case studies are invaluable tools for navigating difficult conversations and establishing boundaries effectively in various workplace situations. They provide concrete examples of challenges that managers and employees may encounter and insights into how these challenges can be addressed and resolved.

Here are some potential real-life scenarios;

Case Study 1: Managing Expectations with a High-performing Employee.

In many workplaces, high-performing employees are valuable assets who consistently exceed expectations and deliver exceptional results. However, managing the expectations of such employees can present unique challenges. While their dedication and drive contribute to the team or organization's success, ensuring that their workload remains sustainable and they receive the support needed to maintain their performance levels without experiencing burnout is crucial.

In this case study, let's consider Sarah, a high-performing employee known for her exceptional work ethic and ability to deliver outstanding results consistently. Sarah takes pride in her work and often goes above and beyond to meet deadlines and exceed expectations. However, her dedication has led to a pattern of working long hours and taking on additional tasks beyond her job description.

Challenges

- **Work-Life Balance**: Sarah's commitment to her work has led to a lack of balance between her professional and personal life, increasing the risk of burnout and impacting her overall well-being.

- **Sustainability**: While Sarah's high performance is commendable, there's a concern about the sustainability of her current workload and whether she can maintain her productivity levels in the long term without experiencing fatigue or diminishing returns.

- **Expectations Management**: As a manager, I need to manage Sarah's expectations regarding workload, career progression, and recognition while ensuring that her contributions are valued and appreciated.

Approach

- **Initiate a Conversation**: The first step is to schedule a one-on-one meeting with Sarah to discuss her performance, contributions, and well-being. This provides an opportunity to express appreciation for her hard work while addressing concerns about her workload and work-life balance.

- **Acknowledge Achievements**: During the meeting, acknowledge Sarah's achievements and contributions to the team or organization. Recognize her dedication and the positive impact of her work on team performance and overall success.

- **Express Concerns**: Express concerns about Sarah's well-being and the sustainability of her current workload. Share observations about her working hours and workload, highlighting the importance of maintaining a healthy work-life balance.

- **Set Clear Expectations**: Clearly outline expectations regarding workload, working hours, and boundaries. Emphasize the importance of prioritizing tasks, delegating when necessary, and seeking support or guidance when feeling overwhelmed.

- **Offer Support**: Offer support and resources to help Sarah manage her workload more effectively. This could include providing additional training or development opportunities, offering assistance with task prioritization, or exploring options for workload redistribution.

- **Encourage Open Communication**: Encourage Sarah to communicate openly about any challenges or concerns she may be facing. Create a supportive environment where she feels comfortable discussing workload issues, seeking feedback, and requesting assistance when needed.

- **Monitor Progress**: Regularly check in with Sarah to monitor her progress, address any challenges that arise, and provide ongoing support and guidance. Celebrate achievements and milestones to reinforce positive behaviors and maintain motivation.

By initiating a proactive conversation and addressing concerns about workload and work-life balance, the manager can help Sarah maintain her high performance while ensuring her well-being and job satisfaction. Through ongoing support, clear expectations, and open communication, Sarah can continue to excel in her role while maintaining a healthy work-life balance and avoiding burnout. This approach benefits Sarah as an individual and contributes to a positive and productive work environment for the entire team.

Case Study 2: Dealing with Persistent Requests for Exceptions.

In any workplace, managers may encounter situations where employees persistently request exceptions to established policies, procedures, or expectations. While occasional flexibility may be warranted in certain circumstances, repeated requests for exceptions can pose challenges in maintaining consistency, fairness, and adherence to organizational standards.

Consider a scenario where a team member, let's call her Emily, consistently requests exceptions to deadlines, work hours, or other established guidelines. Despite being aware of the organizational policies and expectations, Emily frequently seeks special treatment due to personal reasons or perceived extenuating circumstances.

Challenges

- **Consistency**: Addressing persistent requests for exceptions while maintaining consistency and fairness across the team can be challenging. Granting special treatment to one employee may create resentment or dissatisfaction among others.

- **Productivity**: Constantly accommodating exceptions to established procedures or deadlines may disrupt workflow and impact team productivity. It can also set unrealistic expectations and erode accountability within the team.

- **Employee Morale**: Allowing persistent requests for exceptions without clear justification may lead to perceptions of favoritism or unfair treatment among team members, affecting morale and team dynamics.

Approach

- **Open Dialogue**: Initiate a private conversation with Emily to discuss her persistent requests for exceptions. Approach the discussion with empathy and a genuine desire to understand her concerns and motivations.

- **Clarify Expectations**: Clearly communicate the organizational policies, procedures, and expectations regarding deadlines, work hours, or other relevant areas. Reinforce the importance of consistency and fairness in applying these guidelines.

- **Explore Reasons**: Listen actively to Emily's reasons for seeking exceptions and explore the underlying issues or challenges she may be facing. Offer support and guidance in finding alternative solutions that align with organizational standards.

- **Evaluate Justifications**: Evaluate the validity of Emily's justifications for requesting exceptions. Determine whether they stem from genuine extenuating circumstances or reflect a behavior pattern that requires addressing.

- **Discuss Impact**: Discuss the potential impact of accommodating persistent requests for exceptions on team dynamics, productivity, and morale. Help Emily understand the importance of adhering to established guidelines while balancing individual needs with organizational priorities.

- **Set Boundaries**: Clearly outline the boundaries regarding exceptions and the process for requesting them. Emphasize that exceptions will be considered on a case-by-case basis, with careful consideration given to the impact on the team and organizational goals.

- **Provide Alternatives**: Offer alternative solutions or accommodations that may address Emily's concerns without deviating from organizational standards. Encourage proactive problem-solving and collaboration in finding mutually acceptable solutions.

- **Monitor Progress**: Monitor Emily's behavior and adherence to established guidelines following the discussion. Provide feedback and guidance as needed to reinforce expectations and address any recurring issues promptly.

By engaging in open dialogue, clarifying expectations, and exploring alternatives, the manager can help Emily understand the importance of adhering to established guidelines while addressing her concerns effectively. Setting clear boundaries, providing support, and monitoring progress can help mitigate the impact of persistent requests for exceptions on team dynamics and productivity.

Case Study 3: Addressing Boundary Violations in the Workplace

Maintaining appropriate boundaries in the workplace is essential for fostering a professional and respectful environment. However, employees may sometimes inadvertently or intentionally violate these boundaries, leading to discomfort, conflict, or potential legal and ethical issues. Addressing boundary violations promptly and effectively is crucial for upholding workplace standards and ensuring the well-being of all employees.

Imagine a scenario where a colleague, let's call him John, consistently crosses personal boundaries by making inappropriate comments or engaging in unwelcome behaviors towards a coworker, Mary. Despite Mary's discomfort and attempts to assert her boundaries, John continues to disregard them, creating a hostile work environment.

Challenges

- **Workplace Culture**: Addressing boundary violations may be challenging in a workplace culture where such behavior is normalized or overlooked. It's essential to foster a respectful culture where all employees value and uphold boundaries.

- **Employee Well-being**: Boundary violations can significantly impact the well-being and morale of employees who experience them. Addressing these violations promptly ensures a safe and supportive work environment.

- **Legal and Ethical Implications**: Some boundary violations may have legal or ethical implications, such as harassment or discrimination. Failing to address these violations appropriately could expose the organization to liability and damage its reputation.

Approach

- **Listen to the Concerns**: Start by listening to Mary's concerns and experiences regarding the boundary violations she's experiencing. Create a safe and confidential space for her to share her feelings and perspectives without fear of retaliation.

- **Document Incidents**: Document specific instances of boundary violations observed or reported, including dates, times, and details of the behavior. This documentation will be essential for addressing the issue effectively and ensuring accountability.

- **Conduct a Private Meeting**: Schedule a private meeting with John to discuss the reported boundary violations. Approach the conversation with empathy and a focus on behavior rather than judgment.

- **Provide Feedback**: Clearly communicate the specific behaviors that constitute boundary violations and explain their impact on Mary and the work environment. Emphasize the importance of respecting personal boundaries and upholding professional standards.

- **Set Expectations**: Clearly outline expectations regarding appropriate conduct in the workplace and the consequences of failing to adhere to these expectations. Clearly communicate that boundary violations will not be tolerated.

- **Offer Support**: Offer support and resources to John, such as training or counseling, to help him understand and address the underlying issues contributing to his behavior. Encourage him to seek assistance if needed.

- **Follow-up**: Follow up with both Mary and John to ensure that the boundary violations have ceased and that the work environment remains supportive and respectful. Continue to monitor the situation and address any recurring issues promptly.

By addressing boundary violations promptly and effectively, the organization can demonstrate its commitment to upholding workplace standards and ensuring the well-being of all employees. Providing support and resources to both the victim and the perpetrator can help address underlying issues and prevent future violations.

SAYING NO TO CO-WORKERS

If you want to deny requests for assistance from coworkers, the same restrictions apply. You should never react rashly or angrily here, either. This will just offend the other individual and spoil the vibe in the team. In the worst-case scenario, you will be permanently labeled as a hot-tempered and selfish colleague. If you are unable (or unwilling) to accept the assignment, giving alternatives is preferable rather than simply declining. Look for a means alongside your colleagues to ensure the work is finished on time. This demonstrates your understanding of your colleagues' situations as well as team spirit.

Let's see various message templates and examples tailored to various workplace scenarios. These templates serve as invaluable tools to assist you in effectively communicating your boundaries and saying no when necessary while still maintaining professionalism and fostering positive relationships with your co-workers.

Message Templates for Different Scenarios

Saying No Politely Yet Firmly

In the workplace, you may need to decline requests or set boundaries with colleagues while maintaining professionalism and respect. Learning to say no politely yet firmly is an essential skill that can help you navigate these situations confidently and honestly. Whether it's declining additional tasks, setting boundaries with your time, or refusing unreasonable demands, assertive communication is key.

You will need to express your thoughts, feelings, and needs clearly and respectfully while also respecting the rights and boundaries of others. It's about finding a balance between being assertive and respectful without being aggressive or passive. Assertive communication will allow you to stand up for yourself, set boundaries, and confidently express your opinions and preferences. Here are some message templates to ensure this:

V1. Politely Declining Additional Work Requests (#056)

Re: Assistance Needed for Project

Hi [Co-worker's Name],

Thank you for reaching out regarding the additional tasks for the project. While I appreciate your confidence in my abilities, I'm currently focused on completing my existing responsibilities within the given timeframe. If it's urgent, perhaps we can discuss reallocating resources or extending the deadline to ensure quality work. Let's explore alternative solutions together.

Best regards,

[Your Name]

V2. Addressing Workload Imbalance (#057)

Concerns about Workload Distribution

Hi [Supervisor's Name],

I hope this email finds you well. I wanted to bring to your attention a concern

I've noticed regarding the workload distribution within our team. It seems that some team members, including myself, are consistently handling more tasks than others. I believe it's essential for the team's efficiency and morale to ensure a fair distribution of responsibilities. Could we discuss strategies to address this imbalance during our next team meeting?

Thank you for your attention to this matter.

Sincerely,

[Your Name]

V3. Handling Criticism and Negative Feedback (#058)

Re: Feedback on Recent Presentation

Hi [Feedback Provider's Name],

Thank you for taking the time to share your feedback on my recent presentation. I appreciate your insights and constructive criticism. I'll definitely take your suggestions into account for future presentations and work on improving in those areas. If you have any additional feedback or specific areas you think I should focus on, I'm open to hearing them.

Thanks again for your input.

Best regards,

[Your Name]

V4. *Dealing with Aggressive Behavior* (#059)

Re: Issue with Project Deadline

Hi [Aggressive Co-worker's Name],

I understand your concerns regarding the project deadline, and I share your commitment to delivering high-quality work on time. However, I'd appreciate it if we could address this matter in a more respectful and collaborative manner. Yelling and hostility are not conducive to effective problem-solving. Let's work together to find a solution that meets everyone's needs and ensures the successful completion of the project.

Looking forward to resolving this issue together.

Regards,

[Your Name]

V5. *Fostering Collaboration and Teamwork* (#060)

Team Brainstorming Session

Hi Team,

I hope you're all doing well. I'm excited to announce that we'll be having a brainstorming session next week to discuss upcoming projects and initiatives. I believe that by leveraging everyone's expertise and creativity, we can come up with innovative solutions and achieve our goals more effectively. Please come prepared with any ideas or suggestions you'd like to share. Let's make this a productive and collaborative session!

Looking forward to our discussion.

Best regards,

[Your Name]

Communicating Dissatisfaction Constructively

There are bound to be moments of dissatisfaction or disagreement in any professional setting. However, how you communicate and address these feelings can significantly impact your relationships with your co-workers and the overall work environment. Learning to express dissatisfaction constructively is essential for fostering understanding, resolving conflicts, and maintaining a positive atmosphere in the workplace.

Constructive communication involves expressing your concerns, grievances, or dissatisfaction respectfully, empathetically, and solution-oriented. It aims to address issues directly while preserving relationships and promoting mutual understanding. When communicating constructively, it's essential to focus on the behavior or situation rather than attack the individual and to seek solutions rather than placing blame. Here are some message templates to ensure this:

V1. Addressing Workload Imbalance (#061)

Concerns Regarding Workload Distribution

Hi [Manager's Name],

I hope you're doing well. I wanted to discuss a concern I've noticed regarding the workload distribution within our team. It seems that certain tasks are consistently falling on a few team members, leading to potential burnout and decreased productivity. I believe it's crucial for us to ensure a fair and balanced distribution of responsibilities to maintain a healthy work environment and achieve optimal results. Could we schedule a meeting to explore strategies for addressing this issue together?

Thank you for your attention to this matter.

Best regards,

[Your Name]

V2. Discussing Unfair Treatment (#062)

Request for Clarification Regarding Recent Decision

Hi [Supervisor's Name],

I hope this email finds you well. I wanted to seek clarification on a recent decision that left me feeling somewhat puzzled. Specifically, [describe the situation briefly]. While I understand there may be factors I'm not aware of, I believe clarity on this matter would help me better understand the rationale behind the decision and ensure alignment moving forward. Would it be possible to discuss this further in a one-on-one meeting at your earliest convenience?

Thank you for your understanding.

Regards,

[Your Name]

V3. Expressing Concerns about Team Dynamics (#063)

Team Collaboration and Communication

Hi Team,

I hope you're all doing well. Lately, I've noticed some challenges in our team dynamics, particularly regarding communication and collaboration. While I believe we all have the best intentions, it's essential for us to address any issues that may hinder our collective success. I propose scheduling a team meeting where we can openly discuss our experiences, concerns, and suggestions for improvement. Together, I'm confident we can foster a more positive and productive work environment.

Looking forward to our discussion.

Best regards,

[Your Name]

V4. Requesting Feedback on Performance (#064)

Request for Feedback on Recent Project

Hi [Colleague's Name],

I hope you're doing well. I wanted to reach out and ask for your feedback on the recent project we collaborated on together. Specifically, I'm interested in hearing your thoughts on [specific aspect or area of concern]. Your insights are valuable to me, and I'm committed to continuously improving my performance. Any constructive feedback you can provide would be greatly appreciated.

Thank you in advance for your time and input.

Best regards,

[Your Name]

V5. Addressing Misunderstandings or Assumptions (#065)

Clarification on Recent Communication

Hi [Co-worker's Name],

I wanted to touch base regarding our recent conversation about [topic]. It seems there may have been some misunderstandings or assumptions that could potentially affect our collaboration moving forward. I believe open and transparent communication is key to resolving any discrepancies and ensuring we're on the same page. Could we schedule a brief meeting to clarify any points of confusion and discuss how best to proceed?

Thank you for your cooperation.

Regards,

[Your Name]

Managing Conflict with Co-Workers

Conflict in the workplace is inevitable, but how you manage it can make all the difference in maintaining a positive and productive work environment. Effectively managing conflict with co-workers involves understanding the root causes of conflict, employing constructive communication techniques, and seeking collaborative solutions.

Conflict can arise from various sources, including differences in personalities, communication styles, work habits, and goals. It can manifest in various forms, such as disagreements over tasks or projects, interpersonal conflicts, competition for resources or recognition, or misunderstandings due to lack of communication. Recognizing the signs of conflict early on can help prevent escalation and facilitate timely resolution. Here are some message templates to ensure this:

V1. Addressing Misunderstandings (#066)

Clarification on Recent Interaction

Hi [Co-worker's Name],

I wanted to follow up on our recent conversation about [topic]. It seems there may have been some misunderstandings or miscommunications, and I believe it's essential for us to address them to prevent any further issues. Could we schedule a meeting to discuss our perspectives openly and find common ground? Resolving this matter collaboratively is important to me, and I'm committed to finding a mutually satisfactory solution.

Looking forward to resolving this issue together.

Regards,

[Your Name]

V2. Resolving Differences Amicably (#067)

Seeking Resolution to Recent Disagreement

Hi [Co-worker's Name],

I hope you're doing well. I wanted to reach out regarding the recent disagreement we had about [issue]. It's evident that we have differing viewpoints, but I believe it's possible for us to find a compromise that respects both of our perspectives. I propose scheduling a meeting to discuss our concerns openly and explore potential solutions that align with our mutual goals. Let's work together to find a resolution that benefits everyone involved.

Thank you for your willingness to address this matter constructively.

Best regards,

[Your Name]

V3. Setting Boundaries Frmly (#068)

Establishing Boundaries for Effective Collaboration

Hi [Co-worker's Name],

I wanted to discuss some boundaries I'd like to establish to ensure our collaboration remains productive and respectful. While I value our working relationship, there have been instances where certain behaviors or actions have crossed the line. Moving forward, I'd appreciate it if we could [specific boundary, e.g., refrain from interrupting during meetings, communicate directly rather than through intermediaries]. I believe setting clear boundaries will contribute to a more positive and harmonious working environment for both of us.

Thank you for your understanding and cooperation.

Regards,

[Your Name]

V4. Addressing Unprofessional Behavior (#069)

Professional Conduct and Respectful Communication

Hi [Co-worker's Name],

I'm writing to address some concerns I have regarding recent interactions between us. It's important for us to maintain a professional and respectful demeanor in all our communications, but there have been instances where certain behaviors have been inappropriate or crossed boundaries. I believe it's in the best interest of our working relationship and the team's morale to address these issues directly. Let's schedule a meeting to discuss how we can move forward positively and ensure our interactions are conducive to a productive work environment.

Thank you for your attention to this matter.

Best regards,

[Your Name]

V5. Seeking Mediation or Intervention (#070)

Request for Mediation to Resolve Conflict

Hi [Manager's Name],

I hope this email finds you well. I'm reaching out to seek your assistance in resolving a conflict I've been experiencing with [Co-worker's Name]. Despite my attempts to address the issue directly, we seem unable to reach a resolution on our own. I believe external mediation or intervention may be necessary to facilitate a constructive dialogue and find a mutually satisfactory solution. Could we schedule a meeting to discuss this further and explore possible next steps?

Thank you for your support in addressing this matter.

Regards,

[Your Name]

Handling Criticism and Negative Feedback

Receiving criticism and negative feedback is a natural part of professional growth, but navigating it can be challenging. However, learning how to handle criticism constructively is essential for personal development and career success.

Criticism and negative feedback, while sometimes difficult to hear, provide valuable insights into areas where improvement is needed. They offer opportunities for self-reflection, learning, and growth. By embracing feedback rather than avoiding or dismissing it, you can uncover blind spots, refine your skills, and become a more effective professional. Here are some message templates to ensure this:

V1. Acknowledging Feedback and Expressing Gratitude (#071)

Appreciation for Your Feedback

Hi [Feedback Provider's Name],

I wanted to express my gratitude for the feedback you shared with me regarding [specific topic or project]. Your insights are invaluable, and I genuinely appreciate your willingness to provide constructive criticism. I'm committed to learning and growing from this experience, and I'll consider your suggestions carefully as I continue to improve in this area.

Thank you once again for your feedback.

Best regards,

[Your Name]

V2. Requesting Specifics for Improvement (#072)

Seeking Clarification on Feedback

Hi [Feedback Provider's Name],

Thank you for taking the time to share your feedback with me. While I value your input, I was hoping you could provide me with more specific examples or details regarding [aspect of feedback]. Understanding the specifics will help me better grasp your perspective and make targeted improvements. Your guidance is highly appreciated, and I'm eager to incorporate your suggestions into my work.

Looking forward to hearing from you.

Regards,

[Your Name]

V3. Responding to Unfair or Unjust Feedback (#073)

Clarification on Recent Feedback

Hi [Feedback Provider's Name],

I hope you're doing well. I received your feedback regarding [specific issue], and I wanted to address some concerns I have about the points raised. While I understand and respect your perspective, I believe there may have been some misunderstandings or misinterpretations. Would it be possible to schedule a meeting to discuss this further and clarify any misconceptions? I'm committed to addressing your concerns and finding common ground.

Thank you for your understanding.

Best regards,

[Your Name]

V4. Expressing Intent to Learn and Improve (#074)

Commitment to Growth and Improvement

Hi [Feedback Provider's Name],

I wanted to follow up on the feedback you shared with me recently. I want to assure you that I take your comments seriously and am fully committed to learning and improving based on your suggestions. Constructive criticism is an essential part of personal and professional growth, and I'm grateful for the opportunity to learn from this experience. Please know that your feedback has not gone unnoticed, and I'm dedicated to implementing positive changes moving forward.

Thank you for your guidance.

Regards,

[Your Name]

V5. Expressing Openness to Further Discussion (#075)

Openness to Discuss Feedback

Hi [Feedback Provider's Name],

I wanted to thank you for the feedback you provided regarding [specific topic]. Your insights have given me valuable food for thought, and I'm eager to delve deeper into the points you raised. If you're open to it, I'd love to schedule a meeting to discuss your feedback in more detail and explore potential strategies for improvement. Your input is instrumental in helping me grow both personally and professionally, and I greatly appreciate your willingness to share your thoughts.

Looking forward to our discussion.

Best regards,

[Your Name]

Dealing with Aggressive Behavior

Aggressive behavior in the workplace can create a hostile environment, undermine teamwork, and negatively impact productivity. Effectively managing aggression requires understanding its root causes, employing de-escalation techniques, and establishing clear boundaries.

Aggressive behavior can take various forms, including verbal outbursts, intimidation, hostility, bullying, and even physical threats. It often stems from underlying issues such as stress, frustration, insecurity, or unresolved conflicts. Recognizing the signs of aggression early on can help prevent escalation and facilitate timely intervention. Here are some message templates to ensure this:

V1. Setting Boundaries Firmly (#076)

Request for Respectful Communication

Hi [Aggressive Co-worker's Name],

I hope this email finds you well. I wanted to address some recent interactions we've had that have left me feeling uncomfortable. It's important for me to communicate that aggressive behavior, such as [describe specific behavior], is not conducive to a positive work environment. Moving forward, I kindly request that we communicate respectfully and professionally. I believe open dialogue and mutual respect are essential for productive collaboration, and I'm committed to finding constructive solutions together.

Thank you for your understanding.

Regards,

[Your Name]

V2. Asserting Boundaries and Expectations (#077)

Expectations for Professional Conduct

Hi [Aggressive Co-worker's Name],

I'm reaching out to address some concerns I have regarding recent interactions. It's evident that there have been instances of aggressive behavior, which is unacceptable in a professional setting. I want to be clear that I expect all interactions to be conducted respectfully and professionally. Moving forward, I hope we can work together to foster a positive and harmonious work environment where everyone feels valued and respected.

Thank you for your cooperation.

Best regards,

[Your Name]

V3. Proposing Conflict Resolution (#078)

Request for Constructive Dialogue

Hi [Aggressive Co-worker's Name],

I hope you're doing well. I wanted to address some tensions that have arisen in our interactions lately. It's important for me to express that I value open communication and mutual respect in our working relationship. I believe it would be beneficial for us to have a constructive dialogue to address any underlying issues and find common ground moving forward. Would you be open to scheduling a meeting to discuss how we can improve our communication and collaboration?

Thank you for considering this request.

Regards,

[Your Name]

V4. Expressing Concern for Team Dynamics (#079)

Concerns Regarding Team Dynamics

Hi [Aggressive Co-worker's Name],

I hope this message finds you well. I'm writing to express some concerns I have regarding recent interactions within our team. It's evident that there have been instances of aggression, which can negatively impact team morale and productivity. As members of the same team, it's essential for us to foster a supportive and respectful work environment. I believe addressing these concerns openly and collaboratively can help us move forward positively.

Thank you for your attention to this matter.

Best regards,

[Your Name]

V5. Seeking Managerial Intervention (#080)

Request for Assistance with Conflict Resolution

Hi [Manager's Name],

I hope you're doing well. I wanted to bring to your attention some challenges I've been experiencing in my interactions with [Aggressive Co-worker's Name]. Despite my attempts to address the situation directly, I've found it challenging to resolve the issue on my own. I believe external intervention may be necessary to facilitate a constructive dialogue and find a resolution that benefits everyone involved. Would you be available to discuss this further and explore possible next steps?

Thank you for your support in addressing this matter.

Regards,

[Your Name]

Navigating Office Politics

Office politics are unavoidable in any workplace environment, but they don't have to be a source of stress or conflict. Effectively navigating office politics involves understanding the dynamics at play, building strong relationships, and maintaining professionalism.

Office politics refers to the informal power struggles, alliances, and dynamics that exist within an organization. It involves individuals jockeying for position, influence, and recognition, often through networking, negotiation, and sometimes manipulation. While office politics can be viewed negatively, they are a natural part of organizational life and can be leveraged positively to achieve personal and professional goals. Here are some message templates to ensure this:

V1. Addressing Office Politics Directly (#081)

Request for Open Communication

Hi Team,

I hope you're all doing well. Recently, I've noticed some tensions arising due to office politics, and I believe it's important for us to address these issues openly and honestly. Office politics can undermine teamwork and productivity, so let's work together to foster a culture of transparency and collaboration. I propose scheduling a team meeting to discuss any concerns or grievances openly and find constructive ways to move forward as a cohesive unit.

Looking forward to our discussion.

Best regards,

[Your Name]

V2. Setting Expectations for Professional Behavior (#082)

Reminder on Professional Conduct

Hi Team,

As we navigate our work environment, it's crucial to uphold professional standards and maintain respectful interactions with one another. I've noticed some instances where office politics have begun to impact our team dynamics, and I want to remind everyone of the importance of maintaining professionalism at all times. Let's focus on our common goals and support one another in achieving success while avoiding behaviors that contribute to office politics.

Thank you for your cooperation.

Regards,

[Your Name]

V3. Seeking Collaboration Over Competition (#083)

Emphasizing Team Collaboration

Hi Team,

I hope this email finds you well. I wanted to take a moment to emphasize the importance of collaboration over competition in our workplace. While healthy competition can drive innovation, it's essential for us to remember that we're all part of the same team. Let's focus on supporting each other's success and working together towards our shared goals rather than engaging in office politics or undermining one another. Together, I'm confident we can achieve great things.

Thank you for your commitment to teamwork.

Best regards,

[Your Name]

V4. Addressing Gossip and Rumors (#084)

Reminder on Workplace Gossip

Hi Team,

I hope you're doing well. I wanted to remind everyone of the negative impact that gossip and rumors can have on our workplace culture. Engaging in such behaviors not only erodes trust but also contributes to office politics and unnecessary tension. Let's commit to maintaining a professional and respectful environment by refraining from spreading gossip and focusing on productive communication and collaboration instead.

Thank you for your attention to this matter.

Regards,

[Your Name]

V5. Promoting Transparency and Openness (#085)

Encouraging Open Communication

Hi Team,

In light of recent developments, I want to encourage everyone to prioritize open communication and transparency in our interactions. Office politics thrive in an environment of secrecy and miscommunication, so let's make a concerted effort to keep each other informed and address any concerns or issues openly. By fostering a culture of transparency, we can minimize misunderstandings and work together more effectively towards our common goals.

Thank you for your cooperation.

Regards,

[Your Name]

Declining to Take on Tasks Outside Your Expertise

In today's dynamic work environment, professionals often face a multitude of tasks and responsibilities. While the willingness to collaborate and assist colleagues is highly valued, there are instances where individuals may be asked to take on tasks that fall outside their area of expertise. Effectively navigating these situations requires a delicate balance of honesty, professionalism, and assertiveness.

Before accepting or declining any task, it's crucial to acknowledge the significance of understanding your expertise. Each professional brings unique skills, experiences, and knowledge to the table. This self-awareness is the cornerstone of making informed decisions about which tasks to accept and which to decline, thereby upholding your professional integrity. Here are some message templates to navigate this:

V1. Direct Refusal (#086)

Re: Assistance Needed with [Task]

Hi [Co-worker's Name],

Thank you for reaching out to me regarding [the task]. After reviewing the requirements, I believe it falls outside my area of expertise. I want to ensure that the project receives the attention it deserves, so I would recommend finding someone with more experience in [specific area] to handle it effectively.

Let me know if I can assist you in any other way or help in finding the right person for the job.

Best regards,

[Your Name]

V2. Redirecting to the Appropriate Person (#087)

Re: Assistance Needed with [Task]

Hi [Co-worker's Name],

I appreciate you considering me for [the task]. However, my expertise lies in [your area of expertise], and I believe the project would benefit from someone with more knowledge in [specific area]. I would recommend reaching out to [Name of colleague or department] who specializes in this field and could provide the expertise needed to ensure its success.

Please feel free to let me know if I can offer any guidance in finding the right person or provide additional support in any other capacity.

Best regards,

[Your Name]

V3. Suggesting an Alternative Solution (#088)

Re: Assistance Needed with [Task]

Hi [Co-worker's Name],

Thank you for thinking of me for [the task]. While I appreciate the opportunity, I must admit that it's not within my area of expertise. However, I believe [Name of another colleague or department] would be better suited for this project due to their extensive experience in [specific area].

I'm more than happy to provide support in other ways or offer guidance on how to proceed with finding the right person for the job.

Best regards,

[Your Name]

V4. Polite Decline with Explanation (#089)

Re: Assistance Needed with [Task]

Hi [Co-worker's Name],

I hope you're doing well. Thank you for considering me for [the task]. After careful consideration, I've realized that [the task] requires a skill set that is not within my expertise. I want to ensure the project's success, so I believe it's best if someone with more experience in [specific area] takes the lead.

Please don't hesitate to reach out if you need assistance with other tasks or if there's anything else I can support you with.

Warm regards,

[Your Name]

V5. Expressing Confidence in Others (#090)

Re: Assistance Needed with [Task]

Hi [Co-worker's Name],

I appreciate you thinking of me for [the task]. However, I believe there are individuals within our team who are better equipped to handle tasks related to [specific area]. I suggest considering [Name of colleague or department], who has demonstrated expertise in this domain and would be able to deliver exceptional results.

Please let me know if there's anything else I can assist you with or if you need help finding the right person for the job.

Best regards,

[Your Name]

Refusing to Cover for Co-Worker's Responsibilities

Sometimes, professionals may find themselves asked to cover for a co-worker's responsibilities, a situation that requires careful consideration and tactful navigation. Effectively declining such requests while maintaining professionalism is crucial to preserving individual boundaries and fostering a workplace culture of accountability and mutual respect.

It's essential to understand the significance of professional boundaries. Each individual has their own set of responsibilities and workload, carefully crafted to align with their expertise and role within the organization. When asked to cover for a co-worker's responsibilities, it can disrupt this balance and potentially overburden the individual, leading to decreased productivity and job satisfaction. Here are some message templates to navigate this:

V1. Direct Refusal (#091)

Re: Coverage Request for [Co-worker's Responsibilities]

Hi [Co-worker's Name],

I hope you're doing well. I received your request to cover for your responsibilities while you're away. Unfortunately, I won't be able to accommodate this request as I have my own workload to manage.

I suggest discussing your absence with [Manager's Name] to explore alternative solutions for covering your tasks during your absence.

Best regards,

[Your Name]

V2. Setting Boundaries (#092)

Re: Help Needed with [Co-worker's Responsibilities]

Hi [Co-worker's Name],

Thank you for reaching out. I understand you need assistance with covering your responsibilities. However, I must prioritize my own tasks at the moment and wouldn't be able to take on additional work.

I encourage you to discuss this matter with our supervisor to find a suitable solution for managing your workload during your absence.

Best regards,

[Your Name]

V3. Suggesting Alternatives (#093)

Re: Assistance Required for [Co-worker's Responsibilities]

Hi [Co-worker's Name],

I appreciate you thinking of me to cover for your responsibilities. Unfortunately, I'm currently fully occupied with my own tasks and won't be able to take on additional work.

Perhaps you could explore delegating your tasks to other team members or discussing your workload with our manager to find a solution that ensures your responsibilities are covered in your absence.

Best regards,

[Your Name]

V4. Refusal with Explanation (#094)

Re: Coverage Needed for [Co-worker's Responsibilities]

Hi [Co-worker's Name],

I received your request to cover for your responsibilities. While I understand your situation, I can't take on additional tasks as my workload is already stretched thin.

I suggest discussing this matter with [Manager's Name] to explore alternative solutions or adjustments to your tasks during your absence.

Best regards,

[Your Name]

V5. Firm Refusal (#095)

Re: Urgent Help Needed with [Co-worker's Responsibilities]

Hi [Co-worker's Name],

I appreciate you reaching out for assistance with covering your responsibilities. However, I must respectfully decline as I'm currently unable to take on additional tasks.

I trust you'll be able to find a solution that ensures your tasks are managed effectively during your absence. Feel free to reach out if you need guidance on prioritizing or delegating tasks.

Best regards,

[Your Name]

Declining Requests for Financial Contributions or Fundraising

Professionals often encounter various requests for financial contributions or participation in fundraising activities in the workplace. While these initiatives may support noble causes or organizational goals, individuals must carefully consider their own financial constraints and personal boundaries when responding to such solicitations. Effectively declining these requests while maintaining professionalism and preserving positive working relationships is essential to navigating workplace dynamics with integrity and respect. Here are some message templates to navigate this:

V1. Polite Decline (#096)

Re: Fundraising Opportunity

Hi [Sender's Name],

Thank you for reaching out with this fundraising opportunity. While I appreciate the cause and your efforts, I have already allocated my charitable giving budget for the year and won't be able to contribute at this time.

I wish you the best of luck with your fundraising efforts and hope the event is a great success.

Best regards,

[Your Name]

V2. Expressing Support without Financial Contribution (#097)

Re: Fundraising Drive

Hi [Sender's Name],

I received your message about the fundraising drive. It's a noble cause, and I'm glad to see you're actively involved. However, I'm currently unable to make a financial contribution.

Please let me know if there are any non-monetary ways I can support the cause, such as spreading the word or volunteering time. I'd be happy to help in other ways.

Warm regards,

[Your Name]

V3. *Financial Constraints (#098)*

Re: Call for Donations

Hi [Sender's Name],

Thanks for bringing this fundraising opportunity to my attention. Unfortunately, due to some financial constraints at the moment, I'm unable to make a contribution.

I commend your efforts and wish you all the best in reaching your fundraising goals.

Sincerely,

[Your Name]

V4. *Declining Due to Prior Commitments (#099)*

Re: Support Needed for [Cause]

Hi [Sender's Name],

I appreciate your dedication to this cause and the effort you're putting into fundraising. However, I'm currently committed to supporting other initiatives, and I won't be able to contribute financially to this one.

I hope the fundraising event goes well and raises the necessary funds for the cause.

Best regards,

[Your Name]

V5. Encouraging Alternative Fundraising Methods (#100)

Re: Fundraising Campaign

Hi [Sender's Name],

Thank you for reaching out regarding the fundraising campaign. While I won't be able to make a financial contribution at this time, have you considered exploring other fundraising methods, such as crowdfunding platforms or corporate sponsorships?

I'm happy to offer advice or support in exploring alternative avenues to raise funds for the cause.

Best regards,

[Your Name]

Case Studies

Case Study 1: Resolving Interpersonal Conflict

Background: Sarah and Jack, two marketing team members, have been assigned to collaborate on a high-priority project. However, their working relationship has become strained due to conflicting personalities and communication styles. Sarah, who prefers a structured approach to work, finds Jack's laid-back attitude and last-minute changes frustrating. Meanwhile, Jack feels that Sarah is overly rigid and resistant to new ideas.

Challenge: The interpersonal conflict between Sarah and Jack is affecting their ability to collaborate effectively on the project. Both team members are becoming increasingly frustrated, and their productivity is declining.

Solution: Recognizing the need to address the conflict promptly, their manager schedules a meeting with Sarah and Jack to discuss their concerns openly and find a resolution. During the meeting, the manager encourages active listening and facilitates a constructive dialogue between the two team members. Sarah and Jack are allowed to express their perspectives and concerns while also acknowledging each other's strengths and contributions to the project. Through open communication and empathy, they are able to identify common ground and develop strategies for working together more effectively. They agree to establish clear communication channels, set mutual expectations, and compromise on certain aspects of the project to accommodate each other's preferences.

Case Study 2: Managing Cross-Cultural Communication

Background: Emma, a project manager at a multinational company, is leading a team comprised of members from diverse cultural backgrounds. While Emma values diversity and inclusion, she struggles to communicate effectively with some team members who have different cultural norms and communication styles. Misunderstandings and misinterpretations are becoming increasingly common, leading to delays and frustration within the team.

Challenge: Emma's challenge is navigating cross-cultural communication barriers and fostering a more inclusive and collaborative work environment where all team members feel valued and understood.

Solution: Emma proactively addresses the issue by organizing a cross-cultural communication workshop for her team. She invites a guest speaker with expertise in intercultural communication to facilitate the workshop and provide insights into different cultural norms, communication styles, and strategies for effective cross-cultural collaboration. During the workshop, team members participate in interactive activities, case studies, and discussions to increase cultural awareness, empathy, and sensitivity. They also learn practical communication techniques, such as active listening, adapting communication styles, and clarifying expectations to prevent misunderstandings.

Case Study 3: Handling Customer Complaints

Background: Tom works as a customer service representative for an e-commerce company. Recently, the company received several customer complaints regarding late deliveries, damaged products, and poor customer service experiences. Tom is tasked with addressing these complaints and restoring customer satisfaction.

Challenge: Tom's challenge is effectively handling customer complaints, promptly addressing their concerns, and rebuilding trust and confidence in the company's products and services.

Solution: Tom adopts a proactive approach to handling customer complaints by implementing a structured process for addressing and resolving issues. He begins by empathetically acknowledging the customer's concerns and apologizing for any inconvenience they may have experienced. He listens attentively to their feedback, asking clarifying questions to understand the root cause of the problem fully. Once the issue is identified, Tom immediately resolves it, whether it involves issuing a refund, arranging for a replacement product, or providing additional assistance and support. Throughout the process, Tom maintains open communication with the customer, informing them of the steps to address their concerns and ensuring their satisfaction with the resolution.

These case studies illustrate the importance of effective communication techniques in resolving conflicts, navigating cross-cultural differences, and handling customer complaints in the workplace. By employing active listening, empathy, cultural sensitivity, and proactive communication strategies, individuals and teams can overcome challenges, foster positive relationships, and succeed professionally.

CONCLUSION

In conclusion, mastering the art of saying no is a crucial skill in both personal and professional realms. Throughout this comprehensive guide, we've delved into the importance of setting boundaries, understanding the psychological barriers to saying no, and building assertiveness to confidently decline requests that don't align with your priorities or capabilities.

By exploring the various scenarios and message templates provided, you can navigate tricky situations with grace, whether it's declining additional work assignments, setting limits with your boss, or handling employee requests effectively. The case studies highlighted throughout underscore the real-world application of these strategies, demonstrating how saying no strategically can lead to improved work-life balance, clearer communication, and enhanced productivity.

Furthermore, we've addressed the nuances of saying no to co-workers, managing conflict, handling criticism, and navigating office politics professionally and tactfully. By implementing the techniques outlined in this guide, you can foster positive relationships, promote inclusivity, and contribute to a healthier and more collaborative work environment.

Remember, saying no isn't about being rude or uncooperative—it's about setting boundaries, prioritizing your well-being, and communicating assertively. With practice and perseverance, you can develop the confidence and skills needed to say no effectively while maintaining positive relationships and advancing your career.

Thank you for embarking on this journey to master the art of saying no. May you apply these insights and techniques to navigate the complexities of the workplace with confidence and integrity.

Made in United States
Orlando, FL
23 June 2024

48218943R00078